French
INFLUENCES

To Mary Ann —
Vive la France!
Betty Lou
4.11.02

French
INFLUENCES

Betty Lou Phillips

Photography by Emily Minton

GIBBS·SMITH
PUBLISHER

Salt Lake City

First Edition

05 04 03 02 01   5 4 3 2

Copyright © 2001 by Betty Lou Phillips
Photography copyrights as noted on page 159.

Published by
Gibbs Smith, Publisher
P.O. Box 667
Layton, UT 84041

Orders (1-800) 748-5439
www.gibbs-smith.com

Designed by B Design
Edited by Gail Yngve

Printed and bound in Hong Kong

Library of Congress Cataloging-in-Publication Data

Phillips, Betty Lou.
French influences / Betty Lou Phillips; photography by Emily Minton—1st ed.
p. cm.
ISBN 1-58685-080-6
1. Interior decoration—United States—History—20th century.
2. Decoration and ornament—France—Influence.
I. Minton, Emily. II. Title.
NK2004 .P545 2001
747—dc21
2001001921

FRONT COVER: *A solarium suitable for entertaining visiting French dignitaries opens onto formal gardens, which overlook the San Francisco Bay. Cremone bolts are from P. E. Guerin. Absolute black granite paves the floor. The rope handrail is from Houlès, founded in Paris in 1934. The pair of Patina chests were crafted and hand painted in Italy using eighteenth-century techniques.* TITLE PAGE: *With its regal presence and overpowering beauty, a splendid Louis XV limestone façade hints at the graciousness within this* ne plus ultra *of private domains. Rooms brim with imposing eighteenth-century furnishings reflecting the glory of France.* OPPOSITE: *An eighteenth-century dining table and terra-cotta fireplace were unearthed at the Paris Flea Market, though the latter may have been crafted in the Piedmont region of Italy bordering France. (Designs from this region are often mistaken for French.) Host chairs are from Pettigrew Imports in Dallas.* OPPOSITE CONTENTS PAGE: *In a salute to France, a library with a bounty of architectural assets and gilt-edged paintings exudes enviable artistry. Prima Seta silk taffeta curtains hang as luxuriously as well-cut couture gowns, each elegantly fastened by a Niermann Weeks's acanthus leaf. A pair of eighteenth-century French chairs is dressed in a Pollack & Associates woven fabric. The early-nineteenth-century Louis XV desk is from Joyce Horn Antiques, Houston.* ENDSHEETS: *A sampling of "Camelot Medium Fleur" wallcovering from Gold Enterprises, Passaic, New Jersey.*

CONTENTS

Acknowledgments
8

Introduction
12

Making a World of Difference
16

The American Way with French Style
30

Reflections of Good Taste
50

Fluent French
82

French Class
96

Unmistakably French
118

Vive la France!
134

Garden Shows
142

Designer's Notebook
150

ACKNOWLEDGMENTS

"Innovation is often the ability to reach into the past and bring back what is good, what is beautiful, what is lasting."

—Sister Parish

I am grateful to the designers who allowed us to photograph their work: Trip Ayers, Gerrie Bremermann, Dan Carithers, Sarah Lander Hast, Sherry Hayslip, Muriel Hebert, Beverly Heil, Suzanne Kasler, John Kidd, Bobbie Dawn Lander, Christina Phillips, Marilyn Phillips, Judy Robins, Richard Trimble, Carole Weaks, Warren Wyatt, and to the architects who shared their work: Richard Drummond Davis, Jerry Johnson, Anthony Paskevich, Don Schieferecke, and Kurt Segerberg.

A faïence *urn from the Porte de Vanes Flea Market (in Paris's Fourteenth Arrondissement) is set into a curved niche where it lifts wintertime blues with a springtime show of budding forsythia, though it may hold autumn leaves or pine boughs when the season changes.* PRECEDING OVERLEAF: *Tucked away in charming Gates Mills, Ohio, a suburb east of Cleveland, a honey-colored stone manor designed by architect Tony Paskevich might well be set in a remote French province, or even England. Inspired in part by the refined restraint of a seventeenth-century country house, the exterior is imposing without being ostentatious. The interior is imbued with old-world sophistication, yet stocked with more amenities than most world-class hotels —subtly offered, of course.*

10

Thank you, too, to the homeowners who permitted us behind otherwise closed doors where we could enjoy their gracious interiors, beautiful outdoor settings, and magnificent views: Carol and Steve Aarons, Caroline and Douglas Bailey, Janet and Raymond Brekke, May Beth and Barry Bruckmann, Nancy and Dan Carithers, Sherri and Robert Fleishman, Fran and Weldon Granger, Muriel and Victor Hebert, Beverly and Terry Heil, Elizabeth R. Holt, Suzanne and John Kasler, Sheila and Paul Johnson, Sandra and Tom Rouse, Carole and Gary Weaks, and more.

A warm thank you to those friends who kindly gave their time and energy or offered an introduction or an idea: Muriel Abeger, John Allen, Judy Blackman, Bruno de la Croix-Vaubois, David Feld, Harold Hand, Roblyn Herndon, Marilyn Phillips, John Reed, Terry Rosier, John Sebastian, Shelly Stevens, Jayne Taylor, Medora White, Mike Williams, and Jack Zimmack.

Also thank you to those who assisted with photo shoots: Alfredo Alvarez, Ana Bonilla, Molly Feinour, Susan Grice, Alexis Handke, Jeffrey Handke, Nana Kay Kersh, Margaret Mohr, Punita Valambhia, John Walsh, and Brian Watford.

I am also highly indebted to architect Don Schieferecke, whose talent is matched only by his knowledge and fine taste.

I have true admiration and appreciation for the talented photographers with whom I worked: Emily Minton, Dan Piassick, and Nancy Edwards.

French Influences is also the result of the unfailing enthusiasm and artistic vision of editor Gail Yngve, whose talents helped shape this book as well as *French by Design* and *Provençal Interiors: French Country Style in America*. Thanks, too, to the book designer Cherie Hanson without whose creative vision and design this book would not have been possible.

Finally, thank you to my husband, John Roach, and the family who brightens our lives. Unquestionably, their days have fallen under *French Influence*.

INTRODUCTION

"Style is the
dress of
thoughts."

—Ralph Waldo Emerson

14

*B*ehold the power of the French. As tastemakers, they reign supreme. Famous for their discerning eye and flair for stylish living, their influence knows no bounds.

Traversing time zones and connecting cultures, French influence parades smartly down Paris's fashion runways, sweeps through dining rooms serving the finest cuisine, trails off the drafting boards of knowledgeable architects, winds its way into the studios of top design experts, travels out of art galleries and the shops of popular antiques dealers, until those living as far apart as San Francisco and Saudi Arabia must admit that they are the fortunate beneficiaries.

Appropriately then, we salute *l'espirit français* and approvingly honor her people for their venerable artistry, their painstaking attention to detail, and their impact on the design world where, holding the esteemed position of authority, that influence is strongly felt.

—Betty Lou Phillips, ASID

Author and Stylist

OPPOSITE: *Regal eighteenth-century wrought-iron gates make for a grand entrance, swinging open to legacies from eras past waiting to be noticed. A gilded iron console table, bedecked in its original marble top, toasts the symmetry of seventeenth- and early-eighteenth-century pieces that thereafter vanished. Also stepping out of France is a glamorous mirror accompanied by an exquisite chandelier, insuring a lasting first impression.*

Making a World of Difference

"There are two ways of spreading light: to be the candle or the mirror that reflects it."

—Edith Wharton

18

*W*ith their maddening self-confidence, their superior notions concerning cuisine, and their matchless sense of style, the French have a way of intimidating. But, yes, they can also be inspiring, thanks to the sophisticated, polished way they present themselves to the world. Renowned arbiters of taste, their far-flung influence circles the globe, garnering an international roster of admirers enamored with comfort, quality, and enduring beauty—the hallmarks of French panache.

In truth, it is hard not to fall under the influence of the French, who bring inherent elegance and uncommon grace to everything they do. Inspired by their rich cultural heritage and the breath-taking beauty of their country, their celebrated approach to living, dressing, and dining well is as distinctive as their decorating, which is undeniably the essence of French chic.

Which is not to say that interiors are filled with the expected. In fact, settings are disarming repositories for collective heirlooms, plus an ever-evolving panoply of furnishings indulging individual stylistic preferences, varied interests, and an instinct for defining *bon goût*, or good taste. Despite noticeable differences, however, rooms do share some familiar elements—at once the same and wholly different.

PRECEDING OVERLEAF: *Just like the little black dress, an artfully layered white-on-white palette is always in style. And when bedecked with fabulous old jewelry—whether a limestone fireplace, trumeau, fine tables, or a pair of French candelabras—the look is anything but recognizable. Stunning curtains in fabrics from the Silk Trading Company stand out from the crowd, extending the feeling of spaciousness and exuding metropolitan glamour. In Paris, white muslin slipcovers often freshen sofas and chairs come summer.* OPPOSITE: *A dining room rich in French history offers a visual feast, tempting guests with worldly treasures holding closely guarded secrets. Soft light from the crystal chandelier falls on the silk-cushioned neoclassical bench known as a* turquoise, *from the Old French for Turkish. Introduced during the reign of Louis XV, the piece had a mattress-like cushion, no back, and equally high ends. The landscapes are French, eighteenth-century. The rug was custom made, color-keyed to fabrics in the room.*

There are exquisite tapestries as well as somber eighteenth-century portraits and valued *objets d'art*. There are rock-crystal chandeliers, blurry centuries-old beveled mirrors, and respected well-worn Aubusson rugs, which take their name and inspiration from the French village along the banks of the Creuse River where they were made. Also, there are the essential utensils—from France's leg-endary vineyards to the carefully arranged *batterie de cuisine*—chopping boards, *porte-couverts*, or cutlery holders, richly glazed *confit* pots, and *hôtel* silver from forgotten bistros and bakeries that offer a glimpse into the distant past.

Subtly, elegance mingles with ease as the precious sit politely with the less pricey, the ordinary is arranged across the room from the extraordinary—each attracting interest now and then, though some finer things do demand more than their fair share of attention by speaking louder than others. But even in areas filled with antiques, there is an absence of pretension.

An aviary paradise circa 1875—one that most any petite bird would be proud to call home—sings with style. It is perched atop architectural fragments discovered on a weekend sojourn from London to Paris.

More precisely, modest bits of everyday life—charming plates, revered books, outdated maps, fading photos, wooden boxes, shapely clocks, and freshly cut bundles of the same flower—crowd rooms, effortlessly wrapping them with warmth and adding character. Nearly every setting also clutches pieces of family history with a compelling mix of furniture from various periods, thoughtfully handed down generation after generation by caring ancestors.

20

Antique terra-cotta urns unearthed in a garden shop shore up a titanic glass tabletop in Point Clear, Alabama, where open shutters permit an unobstructed view of Mobile Bay. Panels from an eighteenth-century French screen preside over a nineteenth-century bleached oak buffet with Tang Dynasty horses prancing upon it. Vintage Louis XVI chairs wear Payne plaids. Faux stone walls are the work of English artisan Michael Daly, who resides in London where the owners also have a home.

Much has been said about France's disappearing resources, but one simply needs to know where to look for treasures such as the antique urn, vintage barometer, and Louis XV chairs and table with original painted finish. Together they create an intimate setting.

Indeed, in France, meaning in life is sparked by unswerving loyalty to one's country, a healthy concern for others, and, most of all, the love of family, not from purchasing a park-view apartment in a prewar building or talking about costly new construction, sweeping renovations, and fancy foreign holidays that may be deemed *trop cher* (too expensive). But then, discretion is the *sine qua non* of the French, a trait deeply embedded in the soul, reflecting an unvarying level of discipline.

Is it any wonder, then, that genuine admiration for the French and all they represent has widened internationally, captivating those who look beyond Paris's historic mon-

An eighteenth-century chandelier sheds light on the hand-painted breakfast room walls as well as the table seen on page 38.

uments, beneath its ornamental fountains, and behind its architecturally extravagant stone façades? Or that in the States, where imitation is *still* the sincerest form of flattery, French tributes abound?

Notably, French chic is everywhere lately, in elegant, hand-forged iron staircase railings, sumptuous 100-percent Egyptian cotton bedding, and imported fittings perched on nickel-plated washstands in toile-de-Jouy-patterned powder rooms. But this is just the beginning.

It is also on walls where artisans following the lead of the French replicate rough old-world textures that lie beneath numerous coats of paint, or hang wall coverings imitating paint effects like glazing. It is in *salons* embracing generously scaled French commodes, painstakingly carved armoires, and feather-filled *fauteuils* (armchairs) worthy of standing ovations. Whether inherited or adopted, these prized symbols of urban sophistication anchor spaces with layers of past eras and an élan that lands them on the glossy pages of knowing decorating books and discerning home magazines, such as *Architectural Digest*, *Veranda*, *Southern Accents*, *House Beautiful*, and *House & Garden*.

The American appetite for French chic extends to fabrics as well. Swaths of enticing silks, smart damasks, and relaxed linens, expertly woven in the textile epicenter of Lyon, France, make their debut in rooms where gatherings of smartly dressed women and men in well-cut suits sample canapés at sunset, sip champagne, and share lingering concerns with friends. To their credit, most fabrics host masterful *passementerie*—fringes, tassels, cording, tiebacks, wooden beads, and braids—deftly placed to direct attention to precisely tailored floor-grazing curtains, table skirts, and throw pillows plumped just so.

Similarly, antiques gleaned on shopping forays to the fabled Marché aux Puces de Saint-Oeun, the vast flea market on the outskirts of Paris (commonly called Clignancourt, after the nearest Métro stop), amplify the grandeur of rooms. Meanwhile, glistening silver, fine crystal, crisp table linens, and a striking mix of resplendent china patterns—mandatory companions at every glamorous sit-down occasion as *haute cuisine* worthy of the finicky food critic at *Le Figaro*—nestle in containers being dispatched from overseas.

Banquets of heat-sensitive copper pots and tasteful culinary prints spice up less-formal dining spaces where generous helpings of sought-after *faïence* (earthenware with an opaque glaze) and European-sized flatware grace tables set on hexagonal *tomettes* (terra-cotta tile) inspired by the rich warm hues of the French soil.

ABOVE: *An ensemble inspired by the quatrafoil—a four-lobed ornamentation—in Marie Antionette's Versailles boudoir that was produced in 1895 by Scalamandré for the dressing room in Louise Vanderbilt's New York City Hyde Park mansion.* LEFT: *Approvingly, Beauregard, a Lucas terrier imported from England, surveys the grounds. Louis XVI adored dogs but hated cats.*

Reflecting grand French style is a discriminating assembly of European pieces with provenance. Provenance *is a document authenticating the origin of an antique or work of art, and its history of ownership; it also identifies the experts who have vetted or authenticated the piece in the past. With furnishings of assorted* provenance, *the Biennale Internationale des Antiquaires, held in Paris every other year since 1956, is the most distinguished of all antiques shows.*

Stainless-steel appliances infuse this kitchen with innumerable shades of gray. An impressive range of old copper pots, pans, and molds hang on cast-iron hooks. The dish towels were purchased in the Louvre gift shop. A block of the rue de Turenne, in the Marais, is also a tabletop nirvana.

Salvaged stone flooring laid in rhythmic patterns also proclaims its French heritage, adding dignity to both recently renovated and freshly built *chateaux* with towering windows, lavish architectural detailing borrowed from the past, and slate roofs dotted with multiple chimneys and lofty turrets.

Without question, the influence of the French is at once apparent to those who pass through the heavy noble doors of palatial dwellings sprawling comfortably all over America, awaiting generations to come. The image of French country, echoing the furniture, fabrics, and accessories linked with the region of Provence, has changed over the years, though.

A continent away, many Americans have forsaken not only the primitive rough-hewn finishes tinged with the nostalgia of the early seventeenth century when Louis XIII ascended the throne, but also such Provençal clichés as handmade rag rugs, heart-shaped wreaths, farm animals, and pillows with homespun sayings.

ABOVE: *Filtering the light, lace breezily graces many windows in France. The town of Calais, on the shores of the North Sea, is the lace capital, though Chantilly and Valenciennes are also famous centers.* BELOW: *Looks were often deceiving when it came to the out-of-season fruits and nuts decorating eighteenth-century European tables. Today, a trompe l'oeil plate (hung on invisible fishing line) aspires to fool American eyes. Other* faïence *plates by artisan Christine Viennet of Béziers, France—with figs, olives, and strawberries—nestle among the handsome armoires, commodes, and lighting fixtures at Country French Interiors on Slocum Street in Dallas. Cabinet doors are from Rutt, Inc. The Vervloet-Faes hardware was imported from Belgium.*

28

Fulfilling visions in grand houses and costly high-rises with sumptuous square footage, as well as the more modest *maison de campagne*, or country house, is a revamped treasury of considerably more refined furnishings, tracing assorted influences and periods, at times drawn from the reign of Louis XV, although more frequently from a blur of styles descending from *le rois*, or royalty.

It may seem odd that furnishings labeled Louis XIV, Louis XV, and later Louis XVI more often than not did not come into being during the reign of the king for whom they are named. For this reason, it is more historically correct instead to say baroque, Régence, rococo, and neoclassical when referring to various styles. Directoire reigned in Revolutionary Paris from 1799 to 1804, while Empire style, perpetuated by Napoléon in early-nineteenth-century France, was actually a continuation of the neoclassical style born in the reign of Louis XVI.

European elegance drips from gleaming Waterworks fittings into a cast-iron tub surrounded by crèma marfil *marble, evoking the luxury and international* je ne sais quoi *found in Paris's Hôtel Plaza Athénée, Hôtel Ritz, and Hôtel de Crillion. The latter—with lavish architectural ornamentation—was built on the Place de la Concorde in 1759 for Louis XV.* OPPOSITE: *On a Louis XV petite commode or chiffoniére—chest with four small drawers—rests a sophisticated mix of Louis XVI picture frames found on a shopping foray in France. They have a place of honor beneath* Paris on a Rainy Day *by Etienne-Albert Eugene Joannon (1857–1910).*

Never mind that French country's humble roots are firmly planted in the small stone farmhouse, or *mas*—the typical dwelling in Provence—with charm to spare. Set in its comfortable ways, French country is now a widely accepted catchall term for furnishings alluring, enduring, and in step with the twenty-first century a half world away.

It is not that our long romance with the south of France is over, or even a question of urban elegance versus a penchant for *chic rustique*. Steeped in the splendor of freedom, the boundaries of French country are loosely defined, bolstering views that it is as much for the dawn of a new era as for the vanished past.

THE AMERICAN WAY WITH FRENCH STYLE

"Imagination is more important than knowledge."

—Albert Einstein

32

La bella France is awash in inspiration, a gleaming backdrop for, among other things, creativity emanating from within. The chic Parisian streets, irresistible village markets, and glorious gardens overlooking the Mediterranean Sea rouse bright new ideas in the creative minds of all who find satisfaction in unearthing fresh ways of embracing style. For France is the gateway to the imagination with good reason.

It is not just that she exudes a matchless blend of splendid art and architecture, projecting respect for France abroad. Or only that her people are passports to style *par excellence* with the elegance of the eighteenth century woven in their ways. Nor is it solely the passion that they bring to their personal spaces, making their culturally rich country an even more strikingly beautiful place to live. Rather, it is all of these things that fuel imaginations and set them soaring.

ABOVE: *A nineteenth-century Régence-style commode was hollowed out to accommodate Sherle Wagner fittings and basin. The wall covering is a Peter Fasano custom paper.* PRECEDING OVERLEAF: *A Virginia kitchen simmers with style, thanks to finishes selected for warmth and wearability, not to mention an obvious weakness for French antiques. Bricks frame a La Cornue range, creating a grotto, or hollow. A custom-made walnut table serves as an ample workspace for the cooks and their young helpers. Cabinets were crafted by Kitchen Concepts in Baltimore, Maryland. Recycled white oak floors came from a barn more than a century old.* OPPOSITE: *Reflecting the stateliness of an elegant French château, an entrance hall glows with cool marble floors and impeccably crafted ironwork. Seventeenth-century Italian oil paintings ascend the sweeping staircase, connecting an endless enfilade of noble-sized rooms — all pulled together by designer Richard Trimble of Dallas.*

To say there is something about the lofty standards of the French that is inspiring is somewhat of an understatement. Nowhere is a keen appreciation for what is sometimes called the *art de vivre*, or French art of living, stronger than among Americans, it seems. In the *savoir faire* of the French lies our abiding fascination.

Seducing us with their self-assured approach to design, glamorous culture, and lasting respect for the past, we hold the French in awe, unabashedly elevating them to symbols of taste, splendor, and unshakable stylistic authority.

ABOVE: *France has long been a showcase for culinary talent, but savvy Americans also savor copper cookware and attractively bottled Mediterranean olive oils. The French-based Oliviers & Co. now sells fresh extra-virgin olive oils in Manhattan's Grand Central Terminal.* LEFT: *Doors like these often top the wish lists of Americans building chic French homes.* OPPOSITE: *Denver designer Judy Robins crisscrossed the ocean searching for ways to reflect the taste and lifestyle of clients with a home overlooking Chesapeake Bay. In London, she unearthed the antique marble sculpture at Christie's auction house and the Aubusson pillows at Linda Gumb's vintage-textile shop in Camden Passage. The historic tapestry was gleaned from a jaunt to Beaulieu-sur-Dordogne, France, while the antique lamp was happened upon closer to home, at David Duncan in Manhattan. The table is from Nancy Corzine. A Daniel Duross velvet covers the Randolph & Hein sofa.*

Stepping out of the era of Louis XV is a Provençal antique mirror garnered in London at the Olympia Fair. Also from abroad is the poudreuse, *or dressing table with small drawers, which was expressly commissioned. Knowingly, Madame de Pompadour encouraged courtiers to present themselves at an hour when she would be à la toilette, aware that she looked especially alluring. Although ladies today are not inclined to conduct meetings in their bedrooms or bathrooms, some might be tempted to do so in this stunning bath where a new Aubusson rug from ABC Carpet in New York City crowns the Beaumaniere limestone.*

Not simply satisfied, however, to faithfully copy what we see, we take the liberty of upholding our independence, boldly creating imposing, rather than ostentatious, galleries of personal expression often drawn from thoughts born while picnicking among the sunflowers of Provence or meandering through Paris's magnetic Sixth Arrondissement on the Left Bank just across from the Louvre.

Not to boast, we channel our artistry, energy, and resources in fresh design directions, confidently fusing comfort and glamour with distinctly uptown sensibilities fittingly tailored to the demands of American life. For us, there is no greater pleasure than creating a world unto itself, a blissful retreat bathed in style, function, and well-being, where even Louis XV's renowned mistress, Madame de Pompadour, the personification of royal taste, could reside quite happily.

But even with such opulence about, Madame de Pompadour's ritzy habitat in Paris (originally the Hôtel d'Evreux and now the Élysée Palace, residence of the French president) fails to fully indulge some American passions. What was regal and grand in eighteenth-century France, after all, isn't necessarily suited to our twenty-first-century way of life.

It is hardly surprising, then, that otherwise quiet streets, and ones that generally aren't, are bursting with activity as artisans extraordinaire—architects, contractors, designers, and more—mastermind the removal of walls, raising of ceilings, and widening of doorways, creating the illusion of space, all for the better, naturally. Some renovations do, however, turn out to be even more extensive, posing further challenges to those laboring to accommodate various tastes and wishes while honoring the architecture of the house.

Taking special care, dedicated craftspeople plaster over former identities, ultimately converting areas dripping with age into rooms that once did not exist: refrigerated wine cellars, surround-sound media rooms, and his-and-her libraries that are quiet places to work and reflect. For those who desire still greater conveniences, it is possible to install elevators, artists' studios, separate dressing areas, and fitness centers that do away with the need to join a sports club, to say nothing about fancy country kitchens with commercial stoves or wings for elderly parents, which bespeak a new era.

A morning room takes guests on a decorative tour of the Continent, starting in Florence, former home of the artfully hand-painted table, then going on to France, where the eighteenth-century Louis XVI fruitwood buffet was created in the hands of a skilled ébéniste. *The latter is topped by a collection of Majolica —commonly called* barbotine *by the French —boasting the crackle finish characteristic of handmade pieces dating back to the thirteenth century when Italian artisans first adopted this craft from Moorish potters. The polychrome Chinoiserie tôle tea can displaying flowers is nineteenth-century. All that is missing are the famous macaroons from Ladurée's, Paris.*

No matter that refurbishing generally costs twice as much as new construction and, some would say, takes light-years longer than anticipated. Posh, graciously proportioned spaces with updated wiring and plumbing are as important to our lifestyles today as fluid floor plans, lavish lighting, a bevy of fireplaces, and inviting views. Although, nothing may be more meaningful than a *bonne adresse* in a swank area.

In a period of unprecedented affluence, we hasten to avoid throwing good money after bad. How else to explain hauling away dated upholstery that is not in keeping with the scale of rooms, and instead splurging on goose-down sofas with hardwood frames, eight-way hand-tied springs, tailoring details, and bespoken depths and heights—the reasons why they are so expensive.

For the most part, however, re-covering boldly scaled upholstered pieces with comfort and quality well hidden sweeps fresh life into somber settings. But then, dusting sofas and chairs with meters of

In France, there are flowers everywhere one looks. Gardens are a mix of perennials and annuals to provide maximum summer and fall blooms.

deep bullion fringe and piling on a few showy Aubusson pillows also turns once-ordinary rooms into works of art. In addition, glittering chandeliers that formerly brought splendor to the finest Parisian apartments often cast furnishings in a new light.

Taking a cue from the French, we shun track lighting, agreeing that it can be jarring as well as shed unforgiving shadows on the face. More kindly, we layer flickering aromatic candles amid revered picture lights, quietly lit wall sconces, and carefully placed table and floor lamps with the grace of another time.

Taking advantage of today's creative freedom, Louis XVI holds court on an antique Oushak rug from Haynes Robinson in Atlanta. Fabric from Travers drapes the windows. The coffee-table frame is from Italy, while the planter is eighteenth-century French. The bench is covered in a Brunchswig & Fils cut velvet.

Building upon the legacies of those who came before her, Atlanta designer Carole Weaks resourcefully turned an architectural fragment into a planter and a vintage statue into a lamp, then dressed the latter in a box-pleated shade. The skirted table fabric is from Nancy Corzine. The Aubusson pillows with their tapestry-like weaves are vintage.

The best of France, including this eighteenth-century walnut commode from the Normandy region, now resides in a Stateside home where every element, from the nineteenth-century framed needlepoint to a pair of antique candlesticks, speaks of extraordinary taste.

And though it is said that money can't buy happiness, we take our chances anyway, showing more than passing interest in proud commodes embellished with superb carving and gravitating to centuries-old armoires made from the finest woods. Like generations of Europeans before us, we admire their beauty and value their practicality for storing china, glasses, and embroidered linens, which may help explain why we are irresistibly charmed by both.

From the French we have inherited an affinity for freshly cut flowers, healthy plants, family photographs in favorite frames, and worn leather-tooled books that bring studied yet unassuming glamour to our rooms. A special kinship with our distant cousins also draws us to gracious statuary, antique fountains, moss-covered *jardinières* bursting with foliage, and old iron tables and chairs that once crowned hedged gardens where families dined and entertained *al fresco* in warmer months, with sleepy dogs underfoot.

Always our tastes and personalities are expressed in each detail—from window treatments glossed with tassels and trim to patterned carpets and impressive antiques assembled from years of collecting. Admittedly, an occasional weakness for glitter produces rooms that sometimes out-dazzle those of our oldest allies, predictably raising some eyebrows on the other side of the Atlantic, where critics contend we take a more showy approach to country décor.

What passes for French country in the United States, they say, bears only a fleeting similarity to *le style Provençal*, with its admirable simplicity. In fact, to hear some tell it, Stateside rooms boast fabrics and furnishings the people of Provence would never think of using. There is also talk that American rooms are more cluttered and in need of editing.

True or not, it is certainly fair to say our interiors vary widely, taking shape according to one's defini-tion of style. But even while expressing one's inner self, we balk at gaudy displays of affluence. The fact is, sometimes capturing the image of France—even with all its regional variations—is not enough to reflect our individuality, fulfill our need for self-satisfaction, or give us personal pleasure. Seeing no

In a testament to French design, a sunroom with literary leanings is pretty enough to flow into a living room. A classic red and cream toile from Christopher Hyland covers inviting neoclassical chairs. The nineteenth-cen-tury table is from Parc Monceau on Bennett Street — an antique paradise unto its own — in Atlanta. Exterior awnings help control the light.

Furnishings, fabrics, and art create a master bedroom with its own personality. To make up a bed French style, top the mattress with a quilted, stuffed mattress pad, and then two flat sheets, and a blanket with sheets covering both sides. A goose-down duvet will make it even more difficult to stir from the bed.

stigma in fashioning a more global mix, we turn to the great hotels of Europe to transport us to an earlier era, then scour the streets of Italy and other European marketplaces in hopes of discovering treasures that lend importance to other assets already in our possession.

Given the diverse assortment of antiques from which to choose, it is clear that there is no one way to decorate any more than there is one way to live. Which confirms a sense never more apparent than at the moment: too much of any one Louis is dated. Furnishings in the same wood, and even with the same finish, are a bit too predictable. With this obvious nudge of encouragement, we avoid any nagging regrets, and instead give in to our expressive impulses, stretching the definition of French country by putting our own spin on it.

Fashioning diplomatic ties with a mélange of cultures, we eventually juxtapose hand-painted Italian bed frames, hand-loomed Portuguese needlepoint rugs, and discarded German trunks, brimming with hard-to-resist Hungarian china, beguiling Swiss lace, and English sterling silver, tarnished by time. Living up to their promises, all get along famously with French imports already in place and mingle amicably with glassware produced on the Venetian island of Murano, ribbon-tied paper-covered boxes made in Venice, and folding screens from the Far East, though not necessarily by a direct route.

Never mind that pointedly mixing cultures is an almost unheard-of notion in France, where domestic *objets d'art* are the norm with a hand-painted armoire that happens to catch one's eye, occasionally

A lovingly assembled collection of old children's books, bought one by one or in small groups, are not just lined up neatly on shelves but stacked close enough for a young family to enjoy. A favorite of Louis XVI's, Robinson Crusoe*, is also within reach. The reading stand is from The Gray Door in Houston.*

air-freighted from Italy. Savvy as we are about the ways of the world, it is only fitting, after all, that we sculpt our own artful visions of gracious living, disparate as they may be.

Indeed, what we create are hardly mindless rooms shaped by chic collectibles found abroad. Although few of us can resist hosting, even for a time, fragments of history that belonged to another century, decorating, for us, goes well beyond simply filling our homes with handsome antiques, or even linking the past to the present while dwelling on the future. It is infinitely less stilted and more complicated than that. Full of possibilities, it is a way of imaginatively handling life, of lightening

A sophisticated mix of Louis furnishings shapes a salon with architectural presence to spare. Painting the room with further importance are a landscape of dramatic fabrics, a rug with a subtle fleur-de-lis pattern, and an unseen eighteenth-century gilt-framed mirror.

As homes become grander, dramatic windows bathing rooms in light take French design to exhilarating heights, while finely crafted cabinets and luxuriously textured fabrics with well-defined weaves (from Travers) give family-friendly spaces an au courant *edge.*

In sixteenth-century French convents, nuns carefully hand painted humble tin and metal trays, boxes, and lamps, lifting them to an art form soon known as tôle. *Here, lovingly assembled vintage trays, waiting to be ushered into service, garnish a breakfast room wall.*

everyday trials with unexpected humor, of bespeaking comfort and elegance with a storied mix of old and new, patterned and plain, and precious and humble. Armed with lengthy to-do lists, we work at creating a respite from the noisy world of cell phones, lengthy traffic delays, and the corresponding chaos in a new millennium of mounting expectations, all while seeking the commanding sense of style that we find equally elusive.

Concentrating on the task at hand, we pore over furnishing and decorative-art books, visit museums, and browse in antiques shops. In the process of tackling the humbling chore of selecting fabrics and paints, we discover that trips to design centers often result in confusion. But then, it stands to reason that merging fabric swatches and paint samples will never be as straightforward as pairing Marie Antoinette with Louis XVI. Ultimately, however, we manage to turn out interiors both understated and elegant, which professionals often play no small part in crafting.

At their artful best, settings are extensions of our passions, tying together warmth, practicality, and graciousness while tending to our distinctive needs. For us, the reward of feeling emotionally content is a gift unto itself. Then again, *chambres* that reflect one's comings and goings tell a story that is very French. So what if ours have attitude, foreign accents, and an *au courant* American edge?

Magnificent cranes gather to feed in a curve outside a powder room. In the United States, the whooping crane is rarely seen. Nationwide, they number only 264 in the wild. Sandhill cranes are much more common.

REFLECTIONS OF GOOD TASTE

"Beauty is everywhere a welcome guest."

—Johann Wolfgang von Goethe

52

*M*ention the French and most minds overflow with symbols of French panache: sensuous velvets, leopard prints, silk taffeta curtains, deep bullion trim, and eighteenth-century furnishings—originally crafted for the aristocracy and royalty of France.

To this day, the eighteenth century is thought the most elegant era in European history, with French furniture from this period justly singled out for praise. Oblivious to the political and social turmoil that once surrounded it, French furniture radiates luxury nonpareil and commands a loyal following among top antiques dealers, decorators, and collectors who appreciate fine craftsmanship and have the means to buy whatever they please.

Of course, eighteenth-century French furniture with its diverse regional variety can take many forms—some more ornately embellished than French-country aficionados might choose, others in step with our moods and attitudes.

PRECEDING OVERLEAF: *Paying tribute to Madame de Pompadour's passion for pink, elegant Prima Seta taffeta floor-dusting curtains, lined in a Rogers & Goffigon taupe, provide a gleaming backdrop for broadly striped fabrics (a cut of the same pink, pieced with a white) dressing neo-classical-style chairs in Atlanta designer Suzanne Kasler's own dining room. The ecclesiastical candlesticks, stone finials, and nineteenth-century buffet were found in Paris, arguably the Continent's most vibrant capital. The walls are painted in Benjamin Moore's Platinum. (Judith Leiber handbag on chair is from Neiman Marcus.)* OPPOSITE: *Stone strings—angled members into whom the treads and risers are fixed—ascend the steps. The antique altar sticks and the nineteenth-century tapestry were swept from anonymity at the renowned Marché aux Puces de Saint-Ouen, surely the world's largest flea market. With more than two thousand stalls, nowhere is there more to choose from. As a result, Americans with paltry French language skills commonly seek the aid of a courier for help bargaining and shipping furnishings scratched from wish lists.*

Eminently fitted to grace a royal bedroom, a Patina bed—once a canvas for artists in the company's Italy workshop—invites admiration. It is impeccably dressed in Travers fabrics, echoing the hues of the boiserie. *The antique desk is Louis XVI.*

At the century's beginning, Louis XIV, *le Roi Soleil* (the Sun King), ruled France from the glorious Palace of Versailles, built in the mid-seventeenth century and awe-inspiring in its magnificence. In homage to this showhouse, the king's *maître ébéniste* (chief cabinetmaker) André-Charles Boulle (1642–1732) laboriously fashioned the finest woods into regal inlaid furniture, baroque in its elaborateness.

As if exhibiting proof of the court's unassailable wealth and authority, intricate ivory, tortoise shell and brass, or mother of pearl was veneered into *marquetry* patterns, exaggerating the beauty of each piece. Rich *ormolu*, or gilded bronze moldings and medallions, further defined elegance, offering bold standards for royal palaces throughout Europe while enticing the French aristocracy to mirror the king's extravagances.

Swathing a master bedroom in glamour (see opposite page) are four panels of exquisitely carved boiserie with oval paintings original to the sections. Thirty-nine more panels from the same glorious château now grace a Stateside salon. All were painstakingly restored to their eighteenth-century splendor, then assembled like a jigsaw puzzle by Sebastian & Associates of Dallas, Texas, whose artisans altered those that didn't quite fit and produced missing pieces nearly indistinguishable from the originals.

One needed a title, however, to appreciate the majesty of the tall, ostentatious chairs with upholstered, haughty-looking backs and stretchers reinforcing the legs. Since only the self-indulgent king was allowed to sit in a *fauteuil*, or armchair, there was an abundance of lowly stools and benches—all covered in regal fabrics, including embroidered silk. Shimmering brocades opulently threaded with gold, exquisite damasks, and sumptuous velvets garnished with handmade silk *passementerie* took one's breath away. Famed Gobelin tapestries made in Paris and carpets from Aubusson, Beauvais, and the merged Savonnerie and Gobelin factories added layers of overwhelming splendor to rooms.

A trumeau, said to have come from one of the lesser rooms of Versailles Palace, offers a privileged glimpse into the vanished past, as do other splendors imported from Europe, including the neoclassical tufted bench and embroidered textiles from the eighteenth century, when precious gold thread was priced by its weight. The triangular pillows were made from a Spanish matador's coat.

In a bibliothèque *(reading room) perfect for hosting* déjeuners litteréraires *(literary lunches), it is, of course, easy to lose oneself in a stack of handsomely illustrated art books, or even the fat, centuries-old swatch book with early motifs. Vintage textiles also grace the wall. Couture samples are nineteenth-century, perhaps from Lyon, where some of the decorating world's most exquisite fabrics are still produced on restored eighteenth- and nineteenth-century looms.*

A cage elevator is upholstered in a Marvic Textiles toile—the fabric that best represents the Republic of France. The iron doors are French antiques.

With all of Europe watching, ceilings and walls ablaze with frescoes shamelessly begged to be noticed. Elaborately carved woodwork and paneling called *boiseries*, often gilded or spiced with gold leaf, replaced solid wood trim. At Versailles, the sparkling Hall of Mirrors reflected the Sun King's lavishness. Consequently, baroque-style furnishings became known on the Continent as Louis XIV.

Worth crossing an ocean for is the rare eighteenth-century pantalonnière *—intended for storing a man's pants—not to mention the vibrant Bahktiari rug on which nineteenth-century wing chairs now rest. The coffee table was discovered in Nice, while the heavily veined marble top was gleaned closer to the Italian border. The Empire antique burled walnut piano is of Scottish descent.*

In a flurry of enthusiasm, the painted writing table, chair, and "cartoons" mounted on stretchers and framed were bought at the Paris Flea Market, which attracts natives searching for furniture, dealers hoping to discover treasures that others have overlooked, and designers hunting objects for clients' homes, not to mention tourists seeking garden ornaments. But even if one has no intention of buying, spending a morning at a flea market can be fun.

When Louis XIV died in 1715, his five-year-old great-grandson, whose parents and brother had passed away earlier, became King Louis XV (1710–74). As a result, the king's uncle, Philippe II, the Duke of Orleans, was appointed *regent*, or temporary governor, of France until the king attained legal majority in February 1723.

Accordingly, the transitional period between the opulent baroque period and the less formal rococo era of Louis XV became known as French Régence, or Regency. It should not be confused with the Regency era in England from 1811 to 1820, when the future George IV was named regent and furniture resembled the French Directoire period (1789–1804), with its Revolutionary motifs or the French Empire style of Napoléon that followed (1800–50).

Offended by the unrestrained *ancien régime* and put off by the pageantry of Versailles, the duke moved the royal court to Paris where courtiers lived in *hôtel particuliers*, or private residences suited to a less pompous way of life without

A folding screen displays collectibles honoring its French roots. Plates with humble beginnings underwent sophisticated transformation before being set against a fabric crisscrossed with ribbons.

great fanfare. Perhaps predictably, intimate *petit salons* ushered in an era of furniture lighter and more graceful than the heavily carved baroque pieces of Louis XIV.

Shapely *cabriole* legs replaced straight ones on chairs, clocks, and case pieces—armoires, bookcases, and writing desks that were designed as storage. Sweeping curves and refined flourishes, including foliage and delicate bouquets wrapped with ribbons and bows, adorned the upper sections of armoires.

Rather than resting on their laurels, master cabinetmakers fashioned a low chest of drawers called a *commode*, which differed from the *bureau commode*, or large table with drawers, that was crafted in the baroque period. Then, with a puffed chest and plump sides, the *bombé*, or convex commode, made a grand entrance. Startlingly beautiful wall paneling with softly curved corners also became a hallmark of the French Régence era.

62

Nowhere is the impulse to spoil one's most loyal friend more apparent than in France, though many American dogs may lead equally privileged lives. Attesting to the love lavished on a Wheaten terrier by her adoring mistress and master is a sumptuously upholstered bed decked out in a Scalamandré fabric. (If a bed alone is not quite enough, Allan Mawrer, owner of Denver-based Le Petite Maison, can build Fifi her own château with a copper roof, hardwood floors, and air-conditioning.)

Furthermore, a fascination with the Far East that began in 1670, when the Trianon de Porcelaine at Versailles was built for one of Louis XIV's mistresses, increased. When demand for all things Asian—from silk screens and lacquered cabinets with gleaming varnished finishes to blue-and-white porcelain vases and embroidered hangings—outstripped supply, French craftsmen copied these richly decorated pieces, then added showy flourishes of their own. The look brought together Far Eastern inspiration and Western craftsmanship, creating the foundation for the style known as *chinoiserie*, which is still popular today.

The Régence era pointed the way for the more beguiling rococo period—1730 to 1760—when Louis XV and his official mistress (*maîtresse en titre*) Jeanne-Antoinette Poisson, or Madame de Pompadour, had great influence on the decorative arts. Though public reception rooms retained their sense of glamour and grandeur, family apartments were refashioned into less formal settings where strong colors were replaced with the pastels favored by Madame de Pompadour. With a new reserve embracing comfort, Louis XV sought inviting chairs, rather than stools, and fluid furniture arrangements conducive to talk.

A prominent doorway leading to the master bathroom becomes a work of art that pleases the eye, thanks to a magnificent marble-topped antique Louis XV commode with ormolu mounts, mosaic floor laid on the diagonal, and ebony chairs of unabashed beauty. Sconces from Murray's Iron Works flank the elegant mirror, which reflects an adjacent sitting room.

In a dining room as sumptuously appointed as the famously resplendent Angélina's on rue de Rivoli, one almost expects to see the legendary fashion icon Coco Chanel and novelist Marcel Proust, ex-habitués *of the famous Parisian tea room, which opened in 1903.* L'enfant au biscuit, *a rare color lithograph by Auguste Renoir—of Jean, the artist's second son—adorns the* boiserie. *The sterling silver tea set and bowl are from the House of Buccellati, known the world over.*

With parlor games back in style, a matchless mix of vintage chairs covered in playful leopard surrounds a walnut game table from Legacy Antiques, Dallas. In keeping with French tradition, the grouping, set in a corner, is ideally suited for a game of cards or a friendly dinner for four.

As a result, the King's highly skilled *menuisier* (chairmaker), Jean-Baptiste Tilliard, sculpted a perfectly proportioned, low, curved armchair with an exposed-wood frame, far lighter and less regal looking than any previous chairs. On the seat rail of the *bergère*, he carved a basket of flowers. On its back, he shaped shells and *cartouches*, or fanciful scrolls, which communicated that this chair was not meant to stiffly line the wall but rather to be moved about for impromptu use.

As Parisian chair makers began adopting Tillard's designs, the frames of both caned and Louis XV *bergére* chairs were at times gilded or painted. Upholstered arms were moved back from the length of the seat so fashionable crinolines would not be crushed. When hoop skirts were no longer in vogue, they would again extend forward, but the soft, loose pillows still rested on fabric-covered platforms and curvaceous legs remained stretcher-free. Even centuries later, the rich damasks and velvets favored for upholstery would be seen as the height of chic. Meanwhile, the *chaise longue* (sometimes spelled chaise lounge) emerged as a *tour de force* that Americans would come to behold, followed by the *escritoire*, a small desk with drawers and cubicles also called a secretary.

Eighteenth-century French powder rooms were perfect for powdering one's wig. This regal one, off the foyer, is equally useful for catching one's breath or sharing secrets.

Painstaking carvings on many wood pieces were pulled from all aspects of nature, including shells, fish, waves, birds, vines, flowers, rocks, and serpents. Also, designs were commonly rooted in farming motifs such as corn and wheat. Ribbons with streamers and hearts became fashionable, too.

A neoclassical walnut settee, dressed by Pierre Frey and piled with cushions, is as exquisite as its surroundings. But nothing is more precious, of course, than the couple's four children, whose portraits adorn the room. The settee for two became popular in the era of Louis XIV when it evolved in various forms, including being covered with a canapé. *This one is from Watkins, Schatte, Culver, Gardner in Houston.*

Whether set in a French château *or a home in the States, an elegant powder room with chic antiques exudes unmistakable style.*

By the second quarter of the century, dwellings in Paris flaunted brilliant crystal chandeliers and small, exquisitely carved marble mantels with large mirror panels, or painted overmantels called *trumeaus.* Wood floors were arranged in marquetry patterns or in large Versailles-like parquet designs, then laid with alluring Aubusson or Savonnerie rugs. Whereas baroque style exuded a passion for symmetry, firmly holding that any chair, room, or chateau divided vertically should be a precise mirrored-image half, rococo once again endorsed the asymmetry born in the Régence era.

With a matchless mix of elegance and grace, billowing curtains amid dense folds bring fresh simplicity to a
soigné room, where an eighteenth-century German trunk serves as a coffee table. The needlepoint rug from
Stark Carpet is a subtle color-keyed backdrop for Cameron Collection upholstery.

Not everyone in France, however, was sold on grandeur and gloss. Many people preferred the unpretentious beauty of pieces produced outside Paris in woods echoing surrounding regions. If not quite astounding, armoires and commodes were sufficiently commanding—generously scaled, graceful, and easily identified by intricately carved decorative panels with exacting motifs. Eagles, flower baskets, and garden instruments, for instance, were the favored ornamentation in Lyon, Arles, and Nimes, respectively, where furniture was sturdily crafted in walnut.

Others opted for the unassuming splendor of neoclassical style, with refined straight lines and precise geometric shapes arranged symmetrically. Borrowing motifs from ancient Greece and Italy's excavations of Pompeii and nearby Herculaneum, it was shaped by a desire for quiet sophistication. Wall paneling was no longer profusely carved and ceilings were left plain, while doors, windows, and marble mantels were elegantly rectangular. Neoclassical style became increasingly popular during the reign of Louis XVI (1774–89), although Madame de Pompadour and her brother, the Marquis de Marigny, were first struck by its fresh beauty in the late 1750s, decades before the death of Louis XV.

Today's search for the rare, beautiful, and elusive eighteenth-century antiques often take the most knowledgeable collectors and dealers to major auction houses and exalted antiques shows where

A front door swings open to an endearing sculpture bursting with joie de vivre *and the energy of everyday life. The E. S. Lawrence Gallery in Beaver Creek, Colorado, represents the sculptor Walt Horton. Clairvoyant decorative painter Rusty Arena, of Houston, uncannily created the* trompe l'oeil *apple tree polished with an ombré wash months before the fun-loving family found the sculpture.*

but one thing seems certain: in good economic times, the French are less inclined to part with valuable furniture, paintings, and *objets d'art* languishing faithfully in their families, so fewer belongings come into the antique market. What does appear barely gathers dust, even though prices have escalated as steeply as the stairs leading up to the *Basilique du Sacré Coeur*.

Given the importance that dealers of fine furniture and their discerning clientele have placed on eighteenth-century furnishings, it is understandable that the French bemoan seeing their near-perfect commodes, cherished armoires, and beloved dining tables with one-way tickets to cities in the

United States or elsewhere in the world. Not unexpectedly, they tend to look back nostalgically on the eighteenth century.

More importantly, for years now they have viewed precious heirlooms in the hands of shipping agents arranging overseas crossings as a step in the decline of their country's cultural heritage, a proud heritage they long to preserve and pass on to their children. Determination to prevent national symbols from getting away while still within their grasp leads many to canvass the provinces.

With the rest of the world clamoring for French heirlooms, they zip methodically from weekend flea markets to antiques shops to the auctions held since the sixteenth century at various locations in the Drouot, the bustling Paris neighborhood of temptations. In response to

Amid furnishings honoring Louis XV is a mix of pieces from other eras and places. Definitively Italian is an antique baldichino, circa 1720, that once was prominently displayed on a church altar not far from where worshipers respectfully bowed their heads. The antique silver miniature furnishings wait to be admired. In a nod to chinoiserie, curtains and walls are in a Brunschwig & Fils fabric.

Three wallcoverings —one that simulates filled bookshelves, a brick-red stripe, and another unseen —help define a bar, where seemingly unrelated patterns work together, thanks to the distinct differences in scale. For those who can't get over to France, there are American dealers who can help track down wine paraphernalia. Otherwise, check out Au Passe Partout, located on the fringe of Le Village Saint-Paul in Paris's Fourth Arrondissement.

growing concern that antiques are dwindling, the *Gazette de l'Hôtel Drouot* publishes auction information each Friday for the coming week and delivers it to newsstands. But for Americans, there is a downside: the paper is published only in French.

Fortunately, however, chic French style shaping American dreams is composed of periods other than just the eighteenth century. In our minds, furnishings gathered from various eras make a more interesting statement.

Obviously, not just the French are synonymous with fine taste. Designer Christina Phillips layers nine-teenth- and twentieth-century furnishings with old-world comfort, giving an otherwise sedate study in a newly constructed Louis XIV home the underpinnings of age. Curtains hang from drapery tiebacks rather than rods. They were fabricated by Straight Stitch in Dallas.

An unassuming breakfast room takes its cue from leisurely rural provincial life with rich textures and humble chickens plucked from the markets of France.

Timeworn antiques bring country charm to a breakfast room where the newspaper is read in silence and reclaimed terra-cotta tile hints of long-standing use. The Turkish stove standing in the far corner was rescued from ruin after landing in America in hundreds of pieces. Picking up on nature's motifs is a new Ironies table.

SITTING PRETTY

In the eighteenth century, chic French chairs came in a parade of well-documented shapes and unlikely sizes to suit elegant court life. Still winning admiration in fashionable interiors are the:

Bergère: A low, comfortable, fully upholstered armchair with enclosed sides and an exposed-wood frame. During the rococo period, the *bergère* was most often placed in pairs.

Boudoir chair: A small, fully upholstered chair, alluringly fashioned for use in a lady's rococo dressing room.

Causeuse: A generously proportioned armchair, not unlike a settee with open sides. In the seventeenth and eighteenth centuries, the back and seat often were fitted with Beauvais tapestry.

Chaise á bascule: A rocking chair.

Chaise á dos: A high-backed chair.

Chaise brisée: A *chaise longue* broken in two or three parts, one part a foot rest.

Chaise longue: An upholstered chair (armed or armless) with uninhibited charm—and an elongated seating area supported by six legs.

In a corner of the dining room, a gouache (portraying one of four seasons), a neoclassical-style chair covered in a Scalamandré fabric, and a tôle sconce with beaded light covers—passed down from a mother with exquisite taste—create a stunning vignette, adding to the luxurious feeling of the room. A gouache is an opaque watercolor, and also a popular eighteenth-century oil painting study technique.

Chaise percée: A chair with an opening cut in the seat to accommodate a chamber pot.

Chauffeuse (Also spelled *chaffeuse*): A small fireside chair with a low seat, born in the French Renaissance and useful for nursing babies.

Confessional chair: A spacious upholstered wing chair.

Courting chair: An upholstered double chair or settee, popular in the baroque period.

Duchesse: A one-piece *chaise longue*, resembling two *bergéres* with a footstool in the middle, all supported by eight legs.

Duchesse brisée: A *chaise longue* with a separate footrest.

Easy chair: A roomy, comfortable, upholstered chair of any style or period, which merged the *bergère* and the wing chair.

Fauteuil: An upholstered armchair with open sides, deep rounded back, roomy seat, and *cabriole* legs suited to rococo-period fashions. Arms with upholstered elbow pads called *manchettes* were set directly over the front legs when the *fauteuil* was first introduced during Louis XIV's reign, later they were moved back and the legs were shortened slightly.

Pretty vintage ribbons are in abundance at Le Potager in Fullerton, California.

Fauteuil à châssis: Often called a slip seat since the seat can be removed from the frame for recovering.

Fauteuil à la reine: An ample armchair with a flat back.

Fauteuil de bureau: A desk chair with a curved sloping back, one leg centered in front, one centered in back, and one on either sides of the seat.

Fauteuil en cabriolet: A small armchair with a curved back.

Fauteuil roulant: A bath chair.

Fauteuil voltaire: An armchair with a high back.

Grandfather chair: A liberally proportioned upholstered chair inspired by the seventeenth-century wing chair.

Prie-dieu chair: A carved armchair with a high back, low hinged seat for kneeling, and a shelf-like projection to rest one's arms while praying.

Side chair: A term used to differentiate an armless chair from an armchair.

Veilleuse: A chaise with one high end, one low that was designed for one who looks after or watches over another.

Wing chair: A roomy, high-backed, upholstered chair with wings on either side of the chair back. It was also known as a grandfather chair.

Sunlight pours into a regally furnished entry with Louis XVI pearwood chests, eighteenth-century Venetian mirrors, and seventeenth-century Roman baths sprayed with bouquets of fragrant flowers—one of each is unseen. Adding luster to this entry's sophisticated palette is a runner from Hokanson, Inc.

Neither stuffy nor stiff, a dining room exuding a worldly look presents the best of French, Italian, Spanish, and American design. The eighteenth-century enfilade *—buffet with three or more doors—is French, as is the Limoge china and the Christofle silver chargers. Seventeenth-century candlesticks, Buccellati sterling silver, and Coraggio sheers are Italian. The eighteenth-century gilt-framed mirror is Spanish. New Minton-Spidell chairs, made in America, are covered in Clarence House fabric. Pleasing walls were hand painted by Rusty Arena of Houston.*

No question one could be forgiven for feeling like royalty when sinking into a baldaquin bed as beautiful as this one—crowned with down pillows, Matelassé bed coverings, and Clarence House fabrics. Baldaquin is French for a late-eighteenth-century canopy bed with fabric attached to the ceiling or wall rather than supported by posts extending upward from the bed frame. Windows are draped in quilted fabric from Nancy Corzine, Los Angeles.

A luxurious bedroom is a serene place to unwind at the end of the day, and the sitting area in this master bedroom manages to include all the comforts anyone could wish for: a comfy chaise brisée *for reading a book, a mirrored French chest from the 1940s, and interesting treasures everywhere one looks. Promoting the restful feeling, the walls are washed in a silvery brown.*

FLUENT FRENCH

"*Style is the*

perfection of a

point of view."

—Richard Eberhart

84

*O*ffering no apologies for its stubborn insistence on quality and its appetite for elegance, *le salon* is the picture of old-world glamour. With strong, stately architecture—soaring ceilings, imposing fireplaces, generously chiseled moldings, oak parquetry floors, and *boiseries* (exquisitely carved paneling)—most *salons* resonate with cherished and avidly collected antiques, faithfully honoring the Republic of France.

By all appearances, people spend a lifetime closely guarding their artistic heritage, bargaining over folding screens with painted scenes, precious tortoiseshell boxes, stone urns, candelabras, porcelain, and handsome mirrors that were status symbols in seventeenth- and eighteenth-century Europe and now exalt the grandeur of France.

Centuries ago, *marchands*, or merchants, shared the roles of dealer and decorator. These days many living quarters are still knit together without the help of an interior designer. Given discerning taste, an ardor for collecting, and a certain *je ne sais quois*, the French are generally comfortable with their own design sensibilities.

PRECEDING OVERLEAF: *In the warmth of a restored country house, a limestone fireplace and a trumeau—both nineteenth-century—take pride of place guarded by French soldiers in handcrafted English frames. Curtains of humble linen from Henry Calvin Fabrics fall gracefully onto a sisal area rug. Raoul linens cover the Louis XIV chair and the club chair, sprinkling the neutral palette with shades of leafy greens. Attention to detail is New Orleans designer Gerrie Bremerman's trademark.* OPPOSITE: *A walnut Provençal farm table overflows with a compelling collection of eighteenth- and nineteenth-century pierced creamware, first produced in Staffordshire and Yorkshire, England, where it was inspired by antique lace patterns. Our infatuation with creamware's distinctive artistry makes it highly sought after today.*

In truth, they have a seemingly innate sense for assembling and arranging accessories with flair. At first glance, antiques appear to have offhandedly taken refuge in spots befitting their presence. But on closer inspection, it is clear that an underlying perfectionism shapes most rooms. Those who know how particular the French can be are aware that they leave nothing to chance. Every detail, from the assured use of color to the scale of the furniture and manner in which curtains are hung, is carefully thought out and deliberately executed.

It is no surprise, then, that *le salon* is an ever-evolving work in progress that does not come together overnight. Even while developing at a steady pace, however, it is capable of arousing envy in fellow countrymen whose parade of national emblems pale in comparison, as well as admiration in Americans, who cannot fail to be moved by the way an intense affection for France and a deep understanding of her culture guide French people in creating elegant yet welcoming epicenters of style that define their lives.

Some artists sculpt clay, others opt for iron, but Charla Buck prefers tabletops as a canvas for masterpieces inspired by eighteenth-century furniture designs. ABOVE: *Finely painted bees swarm around a bird perched on an olive branch centered on a Louis XVI-style table with faux black marble top.* RIGHT: *Neoclassical-style table.*

A luminous palette of copper, gold, and cream embraces a spacious master bedroom with unabashedly grand curtains and furnishings keyed to the scale of the space. The Louis XV bed is from Nancy Corzine, Los Angeles. The dust ruffle is skirted in Old World Weavers fabric. Upholstery is from the Cameron Collection, Dallas. An unseen eighteenth-century armoire serves as an auxiliary closet.

88

Drawing from the neoclassical era, a Louis XVI loveseat and chairs vie for the limelight with fragments from long-forgotten lives. In a sitting room that radiates with the pride of a Parisian flat, stylish striped silk taffeta curtains embrace French doors. Rooms always look taller when window dressings are floor to ceiling, and even short windows appear taller when fabric is hung as close to the ceiling as possible.

An artfully fashioned entry brims with culture and charm, as France, England, and China each have their say via a love seat, lamps, and tables, respectively. Atlanta designer Dan Carithers is known for giving settings an international flavor plus adding an unexpected accent. A needlepoint pillow suggests a Picasso sans the details, as it hovers over the diamond-patterned painted floor that is also a masterpiece.

Reflecting the history of France—and a staircase winding gracefully to upper-floor guestrooms—is a nine-teenth-century trumeau parked in the home's foyer.

To this end, family heirlooms—both coveted and less appreciated—step out of their previous lives, offering reassuring familiarity, tracing the glory of the ages, and adding obvious sophistication. Never mind that these legacies—armoires, commodes, writing desks, and tables—might be in need of some pampering; imperfections add to their old-world appeal. And never mind that they are somewhat overwhelming for their new, less roomy settings, since large houses throughout France have with time given way to less spacious ones.

Garland trim, symbolic of the period, drips from a grand Louis XVI console laden with treasures transported from France. Pieces from the owner's contemporary art collection hang above the table, mixing past with present.

With elegance befitting a pied-à-terre *on Paris's Place Vendôme, a plump daybed from the Cameron Collection offers the ultimate place to recline, or to sleep a young visitor when the house is full. Beaumaniere limestone hovers over the Murray's Iron Works table, while an Aubusson from Stark Carpet rests underfoot. The large oil on canvas,* Le Grande Boulevard Sous la Neige, *is by Edouard Cortes (1882-1969); the smaller is entitled* Le Boulevard en Hiver. *It is by J. Lievin, star student of Eugène Galien Laloue (1854-1941).*

En grand or *petit*, it doesn't matter. The size of *le salon* in which guests sit primly on plump sofas and sip tea—as if the focus of an Impressionist painting by Mary Cassatt—is irrelevant. It is the revered works of art, layered lighting, and *objets d'charme* bought in a tangle of flea markets and antiques shops close to home that set one *salon* apart from another in a *château* near Fontainebleau, a gentleman's getaway *folié* in Bordeaux, or a *pied-à-terre* in Paris's ritzy Eighth Arrondissement. Suffice it to say that few people are as fiercely devoted to preserving the spirit of centuries past as the French.

93

Alluringly, heritage furnishings' attention-grabbing presence pushes them into the spotlight, and curiously, even *petit salons* become grander, partly because of meaningful ancestral ties stretching back centuries. But mostly it is because generously sized pieces have long typified French rooms so the eye is maneuvered into enlarging its perception of the area.

Of course, it isn't only timeless beauty that gives a space a gracious air by usual French standards, which are anything but standard. It is also the stunningly woven fabrics, juxtaposed patterns and textures, and exquisite details that harmoniously dress, drape, and decorate rooms. Together they turn even the most modest niches into engaging spots at once elegant and charming.

To create a feeling of intimacy in more-generously proportioned spaces, seating is artfully arranged in undisciplined vignettes where groupings of mismatched chairs encourage serious discussions. From the French point of view, being highly informed, confident in one's opinions, and comfortable speaking out on local and world issues is a point of pride and just as important as being fashionably dressed. In their minds, there is nothing deadlier than a roomful of dull people espousing similar views. What's more, apart from being well-read, men must also be adept at exchanging ideas with women to be valued as guests. The French delight in lengthy multicourse meals filled with conversation, but spirited conversations must also continue after guests leave the table for an evening to be considered a success.

Decorative trimmings—fringe, cording, tape, and braid—add finishing touches to window dressings and furniture in France. Those shown here are from Tassels & Trims in New York City. For a glossary of passementerie terms, log on to www.housebeautiful.com.

A card room stacked in France's favor glows with nineteenth-century Régence chairs decked in their original leather. On a weary Persian area rug from the tiny village of Dorokhesh—which, like all ancient rural towns, had its own characteristic style, colors, and patterns—stands duplicates of an eighteenth-century game table purchased from Orion Antiques, Dallas. The term Oriental originally referred to those rugs and carpets made in the Orient, where the age-old craft of weaving originated more than 2,500 years ago. Today, however, it is a catchall label that includes rugs and carpets old and new, handmade and machine-made from all over the world. New Oriental rugs are produced in Iran.

Comfortably stuffed sofas persuade friends and family to linger in elegant *salons* furnished with grand pianos and boldly scaled mirrors that reflect sophisticated *objets d'art*, softly lit chandeliers dripping with shapely crystals, and neighboring rooms. The gaming tables (*trictracs*) accenting corners sometimes serve as cozy dining tables, with impeccable linens—underskirts that sweep the floors and square overlays color-keyed to the décor—trailing across them, giving the cold shoulder to highly proper dining rooms with Sèvres china suitable for entertaining the country's president.

The good times roll as a hairy poker club—winsome English bulldog, adored French bulldog, dachshunds, and wire-haired terriers—adds a lighthearted touch to a canvas applied to the ceiling of a cozy card room in a decidedly sophisticated, grown-up house. The mural is the work of Ft. Worth, Texas, artist Gregory Arth. The chain is from a chandelier suspended over a game table.

Actually, it is no accident that even modest furnishings have discreet purposes in French homes. Enduring the rigors of playful dogs who have the run of houses, sturdy side tables offer places for wine and a panoply of expertly matched cheeses, generally from one of Paris's sixty-two open-air food markets scattered throughout the twenty *arrondissements*.

Always there are pretty pillows stitched from vintage remnants to rest against, lamps placed where they are most needed, and throws draped seductively over sofas and chairs for added warmth. Ottomans and chaise lounges parked in front of fireplaces present ideal spots for sharing gossip chronicled on the glossy pages of *Paris Match*. With a nod to the seasons, paintings casually propped on mantels become the focus of rooms, leading eyes away from unlit fireplaces stocked with kindling and neatly stacked logs waiting for crisper months.

Saying as much about the French as their fine furnishings is their predilection for beauty, orderliness, and simplicity that flows from a penchant for detail, balance, and harmony.

FRENCH CLASS

"*Detail is the difference between ordinary and extraordinary.*"

—Unknown

*I*t doesn't take much to fall in love with Paris's tree-lined avenues, impressive bridges crossing the Seine River, or majestic buildings wrapping around corners in the eighteenth-century style. But decorating in the French manner does require intelligence, awareness, and passion—not to mention patience and panache.

The French find boundless inspiration in their country's vibrant history. Also, furniture with ancestral ties has long taken a place of pride in homes. Yet it is a bazaar of carefully wrought details that reveal the way they see the world and how they choose to create their own place within it.

History wraps a tony corner of rue du Faubourg Saint-Honoré in the eighteenth-century way. The narrow balconies fronting Parisian buildings are not designed for dining al fresco, but rather for brightening streets with cascading flowers and viewing the French capital's posh shops. PRECEDING OVERLEAF: *Rich brown and glowing yellow create two opulent seating areas in a vast living room where symmetrically placed sofas covered in raw silk lend a sense of classical harmony. A linen area rug, woven in France for Stark Carpet, blankets ebony-stained floors. The chairs are from Gregorius/Pineo. The regal array of personal treasures, pillows, and paintings, including a Miró, indulge San Francisco designer Muriel Hebert's well-known passion for antiques.* OPPOSITE: *In a nod to femininity, a gently scalloped skirt and a channel back create a tailored loveseat of extraordinary beauty. The scalloped period table with brass inlay is also in keeping with the demands of the ladylike study. Jim Thompson silks and Houlès trim make up the table skirt. Across the way is a library with a masculine edge.*

Undeniably, beauty is in the eye of the beholder. And some settings do inspire more awe than others, mostly because there is more to decorating than amassing furnishings with presence. It helps, therefore, to keep some basics in mind when aspiring to inviting and stylish *chambres*. For example, in France the foyer is not a place intended solely for warmly greeting special friends with four kisses on alternating cheeks (starting with the right cheek). Nor is it simply where one leaves an engraved calling card, or graciously signs the *maison's livret d'or* (guest book). Rather, it serves as a discreet introduction to the interior, so architectural details are as gracefully rendered as in any major room.

In some *châteaux*, *bastides* (stately villas), and *hôtel particuliers* (private townhouses) of proud proportions, crisp moldings, seamlessly bound together, frame hand-finished plaster walls draped with dazzling centuries-old tapestries. In others, handsome hand-hewn beams and timbered ceilings emit an air of nonchalance. And in still others, thick stone walls privy to long-hidden secrets form stately archways that define broad passageways between rooms.

Finely detailed hardware, in keeping with the period of the house, bestows added nobility on intricately carved doors that hint at the beauty beyond. At the beginning of the twentieth century, surface bolts and *crémone bolts* that could almost pass for artwork—and often are as expensive—became *de rigueur* on groaning doors and tall narrow windows. However, it is the exquisitely fashioned ironwork outlining wide curving staircases and wrapping interior balconies that merits multiple glances, as might be expected, since the French have long been renowned for their skill in making magnificent objects from iron.

Hand-forged ironwork is replete with details from centuries past. OPPOSITE: *A dramatic domed ceiling, with astonishing plaster ribs and moldings, crowns a sweep of rooms swirling around a center hall with old-world opulence. Dallas architect Richard Drummond Davis designed the unabashedly grand French estate that gives the eye an exhilarating ride up spectacular walls.*

Although they shy away from the showy or the contrived, most look upon even the smallest entry as a mini-museum, paving the way for a welcoming mix of paintings, drawings, and prints gathered for their pleasure.

In the grandest foyers, softly lit chandeliers and slow-burning candles shimmer in outsized antique mirrors hung above intriguing commodes that go out of their way to offer smart-looking ladies a place where they may lay their Chanel, Hermès, and Dior handbags and check their makeup. Unfailingly, the commodes and mirrors merely work together. Given that the French cannot abide matching furnishings that lack character, pieces never appear brand new, nor do they have identical woods and finishes.

Alternatively, a narrow console table may fill the wall, with a painting flanked by wall sconces centered above it. Or a rush-bottom *radassiér* (banquette that seats three) with an unexpected combination of pillow fabrics may offer a place to quickly rest.

Light skims across foyer walls subtly embellished with a classical design keyed to the proportions of the ceiling height and the generous molding.

It is the confident way the French accessorize, however, that draws the most applause. There is the grace of a delicately woven shawl or a quilt draped casually over a table, an intimate crowd of picture frames arranged with unrivaled style. And the effortless way a cluster of antique porcelain plates, decanters, candlesticks, or wooden boxes varying in size point out the obvious: A collection makes the strongest statement when artfully congregated together rather than scattered around the room.

That is not to say that rooms stray toward the fussy or the cluttered. While reminders of the past continuously wind their way into residences, the French adhere to the "less is more" school of design,

Light pours into a reception hall where standards of excellence set long ago still flourish. Ironwork with royal fleur-de-lis is worthy of France; fauteuils easily move about; and generous molding frames impeccably cut, floor-sweeping curtains, calling attention to Houston designer John Kidd's intuitive sense of scale. The eighteenth-century parliament clock was purchased at Brahms-Netsi in New York.

In a home with soaring ceilings, massive walls, and lavish architectural detailing, guests might well imagine themselves in Europe. Yet with the exotic blend of Chinese-export porcelain, decorating inspiration also obviously came from Eastern influences. The fireplace and the light fixtures (see opposite page) are old. The French chairs are nineteenth-century. The rug is a forty-year-old Kerman, a fine Persian wool rug. Coveted by the western world since the late 1800s, the most favored grounds are cream, rose, and light blue with a center medallion and an artful border. OPPOSITE: Textured walls, black walnut paneling, and gracefully flowing spaces lift the ordinary to the extraordinary in the same great room designed by Trip Ayers shown above. The balcony railing was salvaged from a mansion destined for destruction.

teaching us that one liberally scaled treasure can have a greater impact than numerous small trinkets. Apparently, to Napoléon this was evident. Centuries ago, long before our ancestors probably even thought about such things, he raved, "I love antiquity. Everything that is big is beautiful."

As it is, icy formality does not make sense in most homes. Nor do rarely used untouchable spaces reserved for special occasions or laced with red velvet ropes. With family relationships and pampered pets fueling French days, most fabrics and furnishings are suited to *chambres* where both family and pets mill about. Even when rooms exude a glamour few can ignore, children's books, puzzles, and toys are likely to be scattered among the collectibles, as if dismissing the commonly held American notion that fine furniture and children don't mix.

It is said that lavender prompts relaxation and promotes better sleep while citrus lifts depression. True or not, sprinkling linens with Edith Mézard's lavender-scented water leaves them smelling as though they were line-dried in a Provençal field. At Château de l'Ange in Lumiéres one will also find beautifully embroidered household linens.

With laundry rooms coming up from the basement, this once-crisp white ceiling fixture aimed higher, too. Lifting the gloom of washday tasks, it puts an exhilarating spin on Peter Fasano's wallcovering, appropriately named "Clothes Line."

Indeed, fondness for the commonplace, the elegant, and the antique starts young, as children learn that their birthright carries artistic obligations. What this means, they are forever being told while being shepherded to museums, is that they must develop cultivated taste, appreciation of beautiful things, and trademark finesse since they will be inheriting fine furniture. In the meantime, shapely slipcovers that don't cost a king's ransom, yet look as if they might, fittingly skim upholstery, protecting the dressmaker's tucks and folds hidden underneath.

In areas that get a lot of traffic, hardwood floors are left bare or covered with hand-loomed Orientals or inexpensive sisal. Old Savonneries, once woven for royal households, and precious worn Aubussons always lounge in privileged places in rooms with minimal traffic.

Quality matters most. While few passions require as much discipline, restraint has long been the French signature. Most resist bargains and buy the finest furniture and linens they can afford or nothing at all. Traditionally, they also frown on over-the-top extravagances that they cannot justify having in their lives. To their way of thinking, flashiness and pretentiousness are breaches of good manners, so it is inappropriate to surround oneself with costly furnishings that are purposeless.

The French, of course, would never say so, but they believe wealth and discretion go hand in hand. Equating elegance with restraint, they deftly sidestep material indulgences that announce their financial well-being or advertise success. For them, comfort and tastefulness are paramount, not high-priced opulence or budget-challenging ways. In France, discreet luxury is key to achieving a look of prosperity and social standing.

Antique tiles, vintage copper measures, and a crowing Majolica rooster, circa 1860, brings the inherent charm of the French countryside to a Stateside kitchen. Following the French Revolution, the rooster came to symbolize the people of France. Thus, it is a favorite motif.

In a setting exuding good taste, guests feast on old-world antiques posed with French flair. A breezy Brunschwig & Fils check flirts with a stripe and plaid, while crisp heads of lettuce serve as centerpieces at an informal supper party. Reportedly, Louis XIV prompted the fashion for round, intimate tables seating six, where it was possible to not just partake in fine food but also to talk freely without being overheard by the servants standing nearby, since dining rooms were uncommon in his era.

In a room both sumptuous and inviting, a stately Louis XV bibliothèque, circa 1820, plays host to European antiques while serving as a fitting backdrop for facing Summer Hill sofas on which friends and family can share laughs. The bullion is a custom Kenneth Meyer trim. The coffee table from Dessin Fournir merits a second look, as it offers proof that old and new can coexist in harmony. French doors open to a terrace, meandering gardens, and a lovely pool.

Nonetheless, interiors call for furnishings with presence, since this is the scale etched in minds. With large *châteaux* yielding to less-roomy ones, an imposing mix of periods that have been in the same family for generations remain the bedrock of French style.

Putting dignified heroic-sized wood pieces and dramatic paintings in their proper place can be challenging, however, even for the French. Unless the right pieces find their way to the right spots, their compelling presence can disturbingly slant the visual weight of a room to one side. As a result, horizontal lines are broken by lofty plants, artists' easels, or floor lamps varied in height. Balance, rather than symmetry, is the secret behind settings with an energy of their own.

This is not to imply that there need be something in every corner or filling every inch. Some of the most inviting interiors are made up of pieces artfully set on an angle or floated in space, opening up rooms. In addition, it matters not if guests must sit on a potpourri of mismatched chairs. It is the feeling of harmony that is important, rather than sameness, which sends shivers down French spines by offending their sensibilities.

Slivers of the past give the impression that settings have evolved over time, thus creating memorably chic rooms. In a country where history and tradition abound, there is ample opportunity to do serious antique shopping. Little wonder, then, that the French are collectors second to none, a fact that they do not take pains to hide. Aside from the Marché aux Puces de Saint-Oeun, a favorite weekend haunt is the Porte de Vanves Flea Market at Avenue Georges-Lafenestre and Avenue Marc-Sangnier, in the Fourteenth Arrondissement on Paris's south side. Regardless, the French are notoriously hard to please, so only that which they love comes through their doors, no matter how important.

What is unusually impressive is that even the ordinary appears to be precious. It helps that the French hand-paint everything—castaway tables, tiles, and fashionable sisal—with amazing pizzazz. Bestowing personality on otherwise lackluster walls, floors, and furnishings looking for a home, seldom do they leave a flea-market chest or chair unturned. In some spaces decorative painting techniques such as glazing, sponging, ragging, or stippling add interest, while in others *trompe l'oeil* fools the eye. The way the French see it, imaginative ways make settings richer and more inviting.

Supposedly, the idea of setting aside a room for books originated in England during the Georgian era, which is loosely tied to the reigns of three Georges from 1714 to 1811. (The George IV period is linked to Regency style.) The bureau-plat, or elegant writing table on which to compose one's thoughts, made its debut in France towards the end of the seventeenth century. Windows are treated to fashionable Scalamandré fabric, while a Randolph & Hein silk adorns the Nancy Corzine chairs.

Selected with a keen eye: a Portuguese bed, a vintage Louis XV bench, and an antique Persian rug from the Mashad region. A gilded carved-wood lamp wears a custom smocked shade. Fabrics are from Christopher Norman. A trio of European squares rests against the headboard, with standard pillows in the middle and small toss pillows plumped in front.

Textures and shapes play in the light, creating intimate and dramatic interiors as contradictions subtly interact: strong with soft, light with dark, sophisticated with relaxed, sumptuous with humble, rigid with fluid. To be sure, textured glazed walls cast a gracious spell that smooth walls cannot, just as gleaming silks, taffetas, and *moirés* radiate a dressier, more-refined look than nubby textures whose shadows mask the light, making colors appear darker and duller than they are.

Sunlight streams through hand-carved shutters, diffusing the light while casting interesting patterns on a guest room's walls.

The French take a dim view of placing two wood pieces or two objects of the same size next to each other. Strong shapes are repeated within a room, but rectangular forms can also snuggle with round, square, and oval ones.

Always bouquets of tightly bundled flowers shower rooms with color, echoing the rooms' hues. Whether straight from the garden or from local markets, tone-on-tone or monochromatic sprays are the epitome of simplicity, densely arranged *en masse*.

Far from extinct, animal prints make their way between the generous sprays of flowers. While zebra, giraffe, and cheetah prints run wild on both sides of the Atlantic, the French prefer a spot of leopard when pulling together a room. It isn't hard to catch sight of a playful leopard print lounging on a sofa or chair, adding a touch of whimsy without sacrificing a setting's dignity. In 1818, Louis XVIII gave two vases from Sèvres, the famed French porcelain factory founded in 1738, to his brother, who later became Charles X, the last Bourbon king of France. Both featured African wildlife, early indications of the French taste for animal prints.

Whether inspired by the resplendent tones of the land, sun, or sea, room settings echo the world around them. The breathtaking blues of the Mediterranean, the balmy sunflower yellows, the glorious poppy reds, and the shifting shades of leafy greens offer limitless choices. As if this weren't enough, homes extract drifts of color from a patchwork of crops and the rich, earthy shades of ochre, sienna, umber, and terra-cotta.

With the unpretentious charm of rural France, an eighteenth-century farm table rests on wood floors in an intimate space off the kitchen. A charming brown and cream toile covers French chairs from the 1940s that welcome daily use. The baskets are old; the functional and fanciful white "jelly molds" are English ironstone. Also pictured is brown transferware, which has attracted collectors for more than one hundred years.

When a modern-day princess burrows under a feather duvet, visions of Paris often dance in her dreams. Yet there is no fear of losing her way in the French capital's tangle of streets, twisting through twenty arrondissements, *each subdivided into smaller areas called* quartiers *(quarters). Whether thinking about touring trendy Marais, artsy Montparnasse or Montmartre, where Picasso opened a studio in 1904, or even checking to see if the giant millennium Ferris wheel still soars on the Place de la Concorde, she first maps out her travels on the bedside wall. The mattress is Royal-Pedic, the choice of six of the last nine United States presidents.*

With mahogany paneling and other discreet touches of luxury, this bath rinses away the stress of a fast-paced life. The marbled floor — crèma marfil inlaid with serrancolon — soaking tub, and walk-in shower add to the masculine air. A vintage chair, appropriated from a bedroom, holds plush Peacock Alley towels, scented soaps, and at times a good book.

UNMISTAKABLY FRENCH

"What is not clear, is not French."

—Antoine De Rivarol

120

*F*illing empty rooms with shiny new furniture is all right for some people, but not for the French. For them, it is unpardonable to live in a house full of rootless pieces with no ties to the past or any sentiment attached. Furnishings must be as meaningful as they are decorative with layers of history woven into daily life.

Not surprisingly, time-worn *vaisseliers* (hutches), armoires with rich patinas, *chiffonières* (chests of drawers) with original paint unevenly worn, and carpets that are threadbare in places fill proper French-country homes.

Monochromatic storytelling toiles have also been a mainstay of the Republic of France. Nowadays, however, they are no longer confined to boudoirs, or private bedchambers, as they were in the days of ill-fated Queen Marie-Antoinette and her husband Louis XVI. Rather, they run though living rooms, into dining areas, romantically envelop bedroom walls and hug bedspreads, oblivious to how Louis XIV might feel about it were he alive today. Or even in the 1770s when two German brothers began designing and printing toile de Jouys at a factory in the village of Jouy-en-Josas, near Versailles. By all accounts, the Sun King did not approve of his subjects living more lavishly than he did at the Palace of Versailles.

Whereas it would be unthinkable to take a Limoge cup from a room-service tray at Le Grand-Hôtel du Cap-Ferrat that looks out over the Mediterranean Sea, or a silver champagne bucket from Paris's luxurious Hôtel Plaza Athénée with its 25,000-bottle cellar, it is quite proper, of course, to take a close look at this ingenuous window treatment and borrow the idea. The fabric is from Bergamo.
OPPOSITE: *Some rooms are as worthy of remembering as some works of art. The terra-cotta and cream palette of this room brings to mind the dignified portrait of Olga Koklova, Picasso's first wife, whom he painted in 1923. In it, the Russian-born ballet dancer wears a fashionable terra-cotta suit while seated on a beautiful French chair. Although important, the painting is unsigned, as only when sold did Picasso sign his work.*
PRECEDING OVERLEAF: *A grand door opens to a sumptuous, light-filled foyer where a confidante, wearing a Lee Jofa print, is clearly the center of attention. It holds court with an air of authority, while a dramatic staircase rises to second-floor guest rooms with grace and assurance.*

Classic botanicals from the Paris Flea Market look right at home in a Stateside gathering room, pulled together by Houston designer Marilyn Phillips. The Aubusson pillows and mosaic tabletop are old. The earth-tone palette is drawn from the Oushak area rug—an Oriental rug of Turkish origins, geometric in design with a wide border. In seventeenth and eighteenth-century France, piqué assiette, or the art of creating mosaics from shards of broken china, became popular.

"If you accept a dinner invitation, you have a moral obligation to be amusing," so said the Duchess of Windsor. Her words of wisdom share wall space with other equally profound sayings, including "In wine there is truth," which many consider self-evident. Posh French wall panels and the Oushak area rug are from the nineteenth century. Antique chairs are dressed appropriately in a Randolph and Hein stripe and West Coast trim.

As the tale goes, Nicolas Fouquet, minister of finances to Louis XIV, hosted a glittering *fête* on the evening of August 17, 1661, in the king's honor at his newly built Vaux-le-Vicomte, the most impressive *chateau* in France.

Against the backdrop of splendor and beauty, six thousand guests, including the entire royal court, dined, danced, and were entertained by fireworks in the astounding garden *parterres,* designed by landscape architect André Le Nôtre, who would later be summoned to arrange the gardens at Versailles. Following the party, on September fifth (the king's birthday) Louis XIV imprisoned Fouquet for life in what was seen as a jealous rage. The problem was that Nicolas Fouquet was less than discreet. All the elements at the Château de Vaux-le-Vicomte not only brilliantly worked together but also reflected their owner's extraordinary taste.

With its impeccable craftsmanship self-evident, the La Cornue may well be the ultimate gourmet range. The French take their cooking tools as seriously as their celebrated cuisine, which not only expresses the culture of France but also sets it apart from other European nations.

A nineteenth-century French draw table—or refectory-like table with two leaves resting under the center one—attracts attention with its parquet top and beautifully carved apron, not to mention stylish Herand, known throughout the world for fine hand-painted porcelain. The Rothschild Birds' pattern is rooted in the 1860s when birds were seen playing with the Baroness of Rothschild's necklace, which she lost in her Vienna garden.

What better place to restore the body and mind than in a soothing spa-like haven where there is no need to call ahead for an appointment? In the creative hands of Dallas designers Bobbie Dawn Lander and Sarah Lander Hast, a vintage radiator cover was reborn as a painted console for storing an overflow of posh towels. The bench is also antique.

A serene, airy haven with a magnetic bay view is decked out with a storied mix of Percheron toiles, purchased in London. Lit en bateaus—nineteenth-century French boat-shaped beds, similar to sleigh beds—anchor the room, awaiting weekend guests. The painted bench is splashed with a check from the French house of Pierre Frey.

In a cozy red gentleman's retreat a tufted ottoman is an attractive alternative to a cocktail table or footrest and is a landing spot to talk. The ottoman of today is only vaguely reminiscent of the long, backless settee from which the privileged sultan of the vast Ottoman Empire ruled during the fourteenth century.

For those who have taken a shine to French furnishings, let no one dim an affection for the unquestionably chic. Indeed, the following symbols are worthy of praise:

A family album filled with pictures. A majestic walnut armoire. Architectural fragments rescued from the trash. Fine art. **An Aubusson rug that dictates the hues of the room.** Bare floors. A grapevine basket. A deep porcelain bathtub hidden by curtains. A birdcage. **Bistro chairs that proudly show their age.** A *bonnetière* to hold bonnets and family keepsakes. Small books with old leather bindings from the *bouquinistes* along the Seine. **Antique**

An intoxicating, burgundy, hand-tooled leather backsplash infuses a small bar in a French country manor. In earlier times, château walls were often covered with patterned leather to keep out the damp.

botanicals. A traditional Provençal *boutis* quilt. A *buffet à deux corps*. A Louis XV canopied bed adorned with sensuous fabrics. A cachepot filled with plants or flowers. A chaise lounge on which to stretch out. A *chien* (dog) treated like royalty. **An ever-evolving collection.** A palette awash in the colors of France. Plain or fancy chandeliers, wall sconces, and candles casting a serene glow. *Confit* pots. Copper pots and pans—seen or unseen. A La Cornue range—the *crème de la crème* of stoves. A commode with intriguing drawer pulls. **A confidante to seat a circle of trusted friends.** An iron daybed layered with comforter and pillows. Decorative painting—glazing, marbling, graining. Irresistible silver bottles for a dressing table. Embroidered fabric with a botanical motif. Spaces left empty. An *étagère*. European fittings, towel rails outfitted with heated towels, and extendible mirrors in the bath. **Fabric-covered walls.** Unassuming *faïence*. Affordable French chairs. A firescreen. The *fleur-de-lis*, symbolizing royalty and the French Bourbon kings. A footstool. A four-poster bed in the sleeping quarters. Freshly cut flowers. A collection of games, such as chess (*échecs*), checkers (*jeu de dames*) and backgammon (*jacquet*). **Iron rods.** Lace curtains. A lamp shade with sassy trim. The scent of lavender. Leopard prints. Fine linens. Old-world maps. *Matelassé* bed covers. A tall flea-market mirror in keeping with the room's proportions. Open windows, inviting in fresh air. Carefully arranged groupings of art, stacked vertically and illuminated. **A mosaic table top.**

A Napoleonic bee, the emperor's symbol. *Objets d'art* found in Paris. An ordinary wood piece embellished with artful touches. An ottoman offering extra seating. Painted chairs with faded beauty. *Passementerie.* Framed photographs of family and friends. Thriving plants. A portrait of Madame de Pompadour or Queen Marie Antoinette. An iron pot rack. A *radassié* from the south of France. **Sheers or gauzy curtains for added privacy.** The shell motif to bring good fortune. Flowing silk taffeta curtains with an unexpected lining. An Oushak or royal Savonnerie area rug to warm wood floors. Sisal, sea grass, or coir area rugs. **Shapely slipcovers with dressmaker details, such as inverted pleating, scalloped hemlines, bow ties, or tucking over the arms.** An imaginative mix of striped, checked, and print fabrics. Sunlight. A throw with hand-knotted fringe. A *tôle* tray or wastebasket. Something surprising but not trendy. A tablescape, lauding a collection. A tapestry with aging

For centuries, Queen Marie Antoinette was thought to have replied, "Let them eat cake," when told that the lower classes of France were starving and their supply of moldy bread running out. But historians now suggest that she was unfairly maligned. Philosopher Jean-Jacques Rousseau (1712-78) first printed the story in 1768-two years before the fifteen-year-old daughter of the Hapsburg Empress Maria Theresa left Austria to marry the Dauphin of France, the future Louis XVI. LEFT: *Bits of vintage textiles, feathers, and trimmings from centuries past—ones that others chose to ignore—alluringly outfit mannequins in eye-catching finery befitting an elegant home. The bodices, inspired by those worn by Marie Antoinette, serve as the foundation for dinner parties, adding a bit of theater quintessentially French.*

threads. ❧ **Ticking.** A documentary toile. At least one *torchère* (tall hall lamp). An unpredictable mix of textures. A trumeau. *Trompe-l'oeil.* Pleasingly proportioned upholstery. Ornamental urns. Vintage textiles stitched into decorative pillows. **Washstands.** ❧ A tilt-top wine-tasting table with wear and imperfections imbedded in the wood. A Louis XV writing table with graceful *cabriole* legs. Antique tables (draw, farm, Portuguese, and trestle). Elegant wallpaper.

Iron chandeliers twelve feet tall, designed by Cole Smith, Sr., of Dallas, drape a sky-high forty-foot ceiling. Also suspended are banners crafted from seventeenth- and eighteenth-century antique velvets, silks, and wools, in keeping with designer Sherry Hayslip's vision and the proportions of the great room. A resplendent centuries-old Persian Malayer carpet warms the slate floors, while a Smith & Watson sofa and antique Louis XV chairs from Newell Galleries in New York rest upon it. All revolve around the sectioned ottoman by Rose Tarlow for Melrose House. The eighteenth- and nineteenth-century wooden deer heads are "trophies of the hunt."

A pale aqua eighteenth-century commode with prized original paint faces intense competition for the spotlight from the hand-colored stipple engravings gracing a lady's upstairs retreat tucked under the eaves. The irises, by master botanist Pierre-Joseph Redouté (1759—1840), grew among the roses and marigolds in the Empress Joséphine's gardens at Malmaison, in Reuill, outside Paris, where Redouté was the "artist in residence." It was to Malmaison that the empress retreated in 1810 after Emperor Napoléon Bonaparte conveniently nullified their marriage on the grounds that a parish priest had not been present either at the civil ceremony in 1796 or at the religious ceremony in 1804.

After a day at the museum, a stately room with Frette linens—the sheeting used in many European guest houses—offers overnight visitors the kind of deluxe accommodations that they would expect to find at the newly refurbished Hôtel Meurice, looming opposite the Jardin des Tuileries since 1817. The neoclassical-style beds are custom finished. The engaging Schumacher toile was cut and seamed so the pattern matches on the face of both beds, and then banded with an Old World Weavers check, giving the fabric a modern edge. Guest room décor in the home ranges from French country to Portuguese.

VIVE LA FRANCE!

"The streets sing, the stones talk. The houses drip history, glory, romance."

—Henry Miller

For the French, quality is a must. Rejecting the philosophy that bigger is better, or even more prestigious, they instinctively balk at pretension and instead gravitate toward excellence. To be sure, the French readily shun *grande maisons* with rarely used rooms, preferring to spend their Eurodollars on old-world craftsmanship and dignified building materials.

A dormer window found on a foray to Paris was copied down to its most elaborate detail before winding its way into this tall sloping roof, where it was set alongside the original. OPPOSITE: *A comfortable morning room off the kitchen sends a kind invitation to savor a* café au lait à deux *and discuss world issues or a recent trip abroad. Marie Antoinette reportedly brought both the hot drink and the flaky croissant to France from her native Vienna, where the Turks had supposedly introduced them. The furnishings pictured were happened upon in the French capital.* PRECEDING OVERLEAF: *Serious cooks set new standards for the French-inspired kitchen, efficiently infusing a space with all the indispensable requirements of the twenty-first century, plus the charm of an old-fashioned country room so spacious that two people can work together comfortably. An iron pot rack, Viking commercial range, and a prep sink (with a disposal) in the granite-topped island make no attempt to erase signs of modern times, yet are admirable in their simplicity.*

For those with a passion for French architecture, here are some elements worth considering:

Arches. Awnings. **Balconies with ornate ironwork.** Balustrade of hand-carved limestone encircling the terrace. Bathrooms *en suite*, or accessible from the

bedroom. Exposed beams with a former life. *Boiserie*. **Bull's-eye windows,** or *oeil-de-boeuf*. Casement windows. A coffered, groined vault or barrel-vaulted ceiling. Distinctive decorative hardware.

Aged exterior doors. Heavy interior doors. **Dormers.** Glazed walls washed in color. A hipped, gabled, or mansard roof crowned with layers of gray slate, terra-cotta tile, or stone. **Exterior stairs.** Parquet de Versailles patterned floor and/or designs from the Petit Trianon, the Grand Trianon, and the Petit Hameau—the smaller houses on the grounds of Versailles. **A bevy of fireplaces.** Graceful French doors with glass panes. Gesso. Hand-scrapped and hand-rubbed

wood floors, stained dark. Latches. **Natural light**. Limestone or marble fireplaces. Generous moldings. Niches. **Over doors.** Plank floors. Plaster walls. Quoins. Rugged, cut-stone façades. Windows symmetrically set. Salvaged materials. Shutters. A sweeping staircase with magnificent ironwork. **Tall ceilings with medallions.** A terrace. Terra-cotta tile. Tall narrow windows through which stream rays of light.

OPPOSITE TOP: *An antique cast-iron chimera — mythical dragon-like animal — rainspout found in a salvage yard north of Bèziers now spews rain out and away from the foundation of a French country estate on U.S. shores.* OPPOSITE CENTER: *A hand-carved stone putto ("little boy" in Italian) — is tucked into an upstairs niche of a French country dwelling where he looks very much at home. Putti (plural) are often seen in Italian Renaissance paintings.* OPPOSITE BOTTOM: *Finely crafted Vervloet-Faes dull nickel hardware, faithful to the past, makes for a gala opening. The passage set, fashioned in Belgium for E. R. Butler, New York, is in keeping with the proportions of the oversized boudoir door. Aside from the style of the house, the scale of the door is a dictating factor when selecting hardware.*

Shunning the grandeur of anything more formal, a Provençal breakfast room with painted wood floor is the perfect early morning meeting spot. In the south of France, pots de confit were used for preserving duck or goose for cassoulet. The bottom halves were left unglazed to keep the contents cool when the pots were buried halfway in the ground. Today these old jars, sporting cracks and chips of time, are prized accessories.

For hundreds of years, blue has been a staple in kitchens with good taste to spare, perhaps because the French, like people in other Mediterranean countries, once believed that it would keep all manner of misfortune away. These days, favored blue is still très chic. *Glowing hand-painted tile—reminiscent of Claude Monet's kitchen at Giverny—complements the Wm Ohs'* bombé *cabinets.*

GARDEN SHOWS

"Show me your
garden and I
shall tell you
what you are."

—Alfred Austin

*T*he Tuileries Gardens in Paris, visited by some six million people annually, are a monument to French ways. Designed by the great landscape artist André Le Nôtre in the 1660s, the gardens lend new meaning to the love of order. Quiet lawns, stone terraces, tidy flowerbeds, reflecting pools supplied by aeolians, or pumps propelled by the wind, and trees symmetrically lined up like military soldiers protect the sixty-seven-acre gardens from the exuberant city streets.

Away from camera-wielding tourists, private gardens revel in the imaginations of amateur and professional gardeners, influenced by the soil and the climate. With mosaic France stretching from the lowlands to the Mediterranean Sea and from the picturesque Alps to the Atlantic, creating a handsome outdoor setting is a bit of an art.

In France, the wines of Bordeaux and Burgundy are king and queen; Bordeaux boasts more than seven thousand wine makers. Pictured is a new-growth vineyard. OPPOSITE: *Home to frogs and goldfish, a spring-fed lily pond revels in the changing light. It was the lily pond at Giverny that inspired the famous paintings Claude Monet called* Les Nymphèas. PRECEDING OVERLEAF: *The pool house of a French country home beckons warmer days filled with sunshine and leisurely al fresco suppers by the pool. Meanwhile, the wooded landscape is enjoyed from the terrace. The furniture is from Murray's Iron Works, Dallas.*

A long allée *—or parallel rows of trees—with a winding gravel path leads to the unknown.*

On this side of the Atlantic, the soil, the climate, and the sunlight are equally diverse. But it is possible to express artistic gardening sensibility that is worthy of the French by taking a cue from the paint boxes and canvases of the Impressionists that include the following:

An *allée*, or sweeping walkway lined with rows of parallel trees. **Asters.** Azaleas. A stone bench. A birdbath and bird feeder. An arbor or gracious outdoor room. Birch trees. Blue agapanthus. Boxwoods shaped like globes. Butterflies. Camellias. Clematis climbing a wall. Cosmos. **A courtyard with pale gravel or pebbles or cobblestones.** A trio of cypress trees to bring good fortune.

The Marché Biologique, or Organic Market, held every Sunday morning on the Boulevard Raspail, in the Seventeenth Arrondissement, is by far the best-known—and most stylish— of Paris's outdoor markets. An offshoot is the Marché Biologique Batignolles, held every Saturday.

The French as well as Americans often need look no further than their own gardens for ways to glamorize their rooms.

Daffodils. Drainage system. **Ducks.** *Espaliered* fruit trees. A gurgling fountain. A garden gate. Geraniums planted in antique olive jars. Goldfish. Gravel paths. A low groundcover. Hollyhocks. Hyacinth. Hibiscus. Hydrangea. Irises. **Iron tables and chairs.** *Jardinières* overflowing with foliage. Jasmine. Laurel. **Lavender beds.** *Le jardin d'herbes*, or herb garden. *Parterres*, or flowerbeds. Lemon and lime trees. Marigolds. Narcissi. Olive trees in terra-cotta pots. Peonies, the showiest of flowers. A pergola.

A spring-fed pond. Red poppies. A *potager*, or kitchen garden with vegetables and herbs. Roses, lilacs, and lilies. Neighboring rows of same-color flowers—for example, blue hydrangeas, flax flowers, bluebells, delphiniums, and foxgloves. **Statuary in a state of decay.** Terraces. A tool shed. Topiaries set in large planters. Majestic chestnut trees. Trellises. Urns. Hundreds of same-color tulips. **Verdant lawns.** Cones of clipped yew. Stone walls. Water lilies. Window boxes bursting with flowers. Wisteria.

Perched on a sunny terrace, a rooster enjoys panoramic views of Dallas, unconcerned that he is no longer the official symbol of France, as he was in the days of the Third Republic. (However he still stands proudly on the Seal of State, actually dating back to the Second Republic.) Napoléon I rejected the idea of the rooster becoming the country's emblem, saying flatly, "The rooster has no strength, in no way can it stand as the image of an empire such as France." Napoléon III also viewed the rooster with distaste. Since 1945, the statue of Marianne has graced public buildings, symbolizing the people of France. RIGHT: Breakfast chairs awash in a painterly palette are upholstered in fabric. But there is nothing to stand in the way of artistic souls painting their own seating.

An imposing statue that originally guarded an important villa on the sunny Côte d'Azur now keeps a watchful eye on a French estate on this side of the Atlantic.

DESIGNER'S NOTEBOOK

"Go confidently in the direction of your dreams. Live the life you have imagined."

—Henry David Thoreau

152

*T*he search for fine fabrics, furniture, antiques, and upholstery does not necessarily require a trip abroad, as there are excellent resources on this side of the Atlantic, too.

PRECEDING OVERLEAF: *In collaboration with nature, Segerberg Mayhew Architects in Vail, Colorado, turned stone, iron, copper, and sand into a towering* maison de campagne *that celebrates the earth's bounty while proudly following the contours of the land. Taking a cue from eighteenth-century dwellings with large windows and roomy interior spaces, the house boasts a "keep," or tower, thick plaster walls, deep-set windows, decorative ironwork, and wide-plank floors, thus beautifying a family hideaway where generations gather for timeless weekends.*

Aside from combing showrooms in design centers, professional designers are regular visitors to well-known department stores, such as Neiman Marcus, Bergdorf Goodman, Barneys New York, Bloomingdale's, and Saks Fifth Avenue. Also among our favorite stomping grounds are the retail establishments of Pierre Deux, Ralph Lauren, Crate & Barrel, Pottery Barn, Pier 1 Imports, Williams-Sonoma, and Banana Republic. Then, too, we are big believers in catalog shopping with Ballard Designs definitely worth a second look. More of our favorite resources are:

ANTIQUE FURNISHINGS AND ACCESSORIES

Jacqueline Adams
2300 Peachtree Road NW
Suite B-110
Atlanta, GA 30309
Telephone: 404.355.8123

Agostino Antiques Ltd.
808 Broadway at 11th Street
New York, NY 10003
Telephone: 212.533.3355

Brian Stringer Antiques
2031 West Alabama
Houston, TX 77006
Telephone: 713.526.7380

Carl Moore Antiques
1610 Bissonnet Street
Houston, TX 77005
Telephone: 713.524.2502

Charles Gaylord Antiques
2151 Powell Street
San Francisco, CA 94133
Telephone: 415.392.6085

Country French Interiors
1428 Slocum Street
Dallas, TX 75207
Telephone: 214.747.4700

Ed Hardy San Francisco, Inc.
188 Henry Adams Street
San Francisco, CA 94103
Telephone: 415.626.6300
www.edhardysf.com

Fireside Antiques
14007 Perkins Road
Baton Rouge, LA 70810
Telephone: 225.752.9565
www.firesideantiques.com

The French Attic
The Stalls
116 Bennett Street
Atlanta, GA 30309
Telephone: 404.352.4430

The Gables
711 Miami Circle
Atlanta, GA 30324
Telephone: 1.800.753.3342
www.thegablesantiques.com

The Gray Door
1809 West Gray Street
Houston, TX 77019
Telephone: 713.521.9085

Jane J. Marsden Antiques
2300 Peachtree Road NW
Atlanta, GA 30309
Telephone: 404.355.1288
www.marsdenantiques.com

Jane Moore Interiors
2922 Virginia Street
Houston, TX 77098
Telephone: 713.526.6113

John Rosselli & Associates, Ltd.
523 East 73rd Street
New York, NY 10021
Telephone: 212.772.2137

John Rosselli & Associates, Ltd.
255 East 72nd Street
New York, NY 10012
Telephone: 212.737.2252

Joseph Minton Antiques
1410 Slocum Street
Dallas, TX 75207
Telephone: 214.744.3111
www.mintonantiques.com

Joyce Horn Antiques
1008 Wirt Road
Houston, TX 77055
Telephone: 713.688.0507

Junque
2303 A Dunlavy Street
Houston, TX 77006
Telephone: 713.529.2177

Inessa Stewart Antiques
8630 Perkins Road
Baton Rouge, LA 70810
Telephone: 225.769.9363

Inessa Stewart Antiques
5201 West Lovers Lane
Dallas, TX 75209
Telephone: 214.366.2660

Le Louvre
1313 Slocum Street
Dallas, TX 75207
Telephone: 214.752.2605

Legacy Antiques
1406 Slocum Street
Dallas, TX 75207
Telephone: 214.748.4606

The Lotus Collection
445 Jackson Street
San Francisco, CA 94111
Telephone: 415.398.8115

Made In France
2912 Ferndale Place
Houston, TX 77098
Telephone: 713.529.7949

The Mews
1708 Market Center Boulevard
Dallas, TX 75207
Telephone: 214.748.9070

Newell Art Galleries, Inc.
425 East 53rd Street
New York, NY 10022
Telephone: 212.758.1970
www.newell.com

Nick Brock, Antiques
2909 North Henderson Street
Dallas, TX 75206
Telephone: 214.828.0624

Orion Antique Importers, Inc.
1435 Slocum Street
Dallas, TX 75207
Telephone: 214.748.1177

Parc Monceau
45-D NW Bennett Street
Atlanta, GA 30309
Telephone: 404.355.3766

Uncommon Market, Inc.
2701 Fairmount
Dallas, TX 75201
Telephone: 214.871.2775

Watkins, Schatte, Culver, Gardner
2308 Bissonnet Street
Houston, TX 77005
Telephone: 713.529.0597

Savvy Provençal soap makers are more concerned with the ingredients that give the finished product special qualities than with exquisite packaging.

BATH FITTINGS

Czech & Speake
350 11th Street
Hoboken, NJ 07030
Telephone: 1.800.632.4165
www.homeportfolio.com

Kallista, Inc.
2446 Verna Court
San Leandro, CA 94577
Telephone: 1.888.4.Kallista
www.kallistainc.com

St. Thomas Creations, Inc.
1022 West 24th Street, Suite 125
National City, CA 91950
Telephone: 619.474.9490
www.stthomascreations.com

Sherle Wagner, International
60 East 57th Street
New York, NY 10022
Telephone: 212.758.3300
www.sherlewagner.com

Waterworks
60 Backus Avenue
Danbury, CT 06810
Telephone: 1.800.899.6757
www.waterworks.com

CARPETS

Asmara, Inc.
99 Black Falcon Avenue
Boston, MA 02210
Telephone: 1.800.451.7240
www.asmarainc.com/va.mar.html

Beauvais Carpets
201 East 57th Street
New York, NY 10022
Telephone: 212.688.2265

Design Materials
241 South 55th Street
Kansas City, KS 66106
Telephone: 913.342.9796

Hokanson
Decorative Center
5120 Woodway Road
Houston, TX 77056
Telephone: 1.800.243.7771
www.hokansoncarpet.com

Mark, Inc.
323 Railroad Avenue
Greenwich, CT 06830
Telephone: 203.861.0110
www.brunschwig.com

154

Rosecore Carpet Co., Inc.
D & D Building
979 Third Avenue
New York, NY 10022
Telephone: 212.421.7272
www.rosecore.com

Stark Carpet
D & D Building
979 Third Avenue
New York, NY 10022
Telephone: 212.752.9000
www.starkcarpet.com

DECORATIVE HARDWARE

E. R. Butler & Co., Inc.
Maison J. Vervloeot-Faces
75 Spring Street, 5th Floor
New York, NY 10012
Telephone: 212.925.3565
www.erbutler.com

Nanz Custom Hardware
20 Vandam Street
New York, NY 10013
Telephone: 212.367.7000
www.nanz.com

Palmer Designs
7875 Convoy Court, Suite 5
San Diego, CA 92111
Telephone: 858.576.1350
www.palmer-design.com

P. E. Guerin, Inc.
21–23 Jane Street
New York, NY 10014
Telephone: 212.243.5270
www.peguerin.aol.com

FABRICS AND WALL COVERINGS

Anna French
Classic Revivals
One Design Center Place, Suite 534
Boston, MA 02210
Telephone: 617.574.9030

Bennison Fabrics
76 Greene Street
New York, NY 10012
Telephone: 212.941.1212

Bergamo Fabrics
7 West 22nd Street, 2nd Floor
New York, NY 10011
Telephone: 212.462.1010
www.bergamofabrics.com

Brunschwig & Fils, Inc.
75 Virginia Road
North White Plains, NY 10603
Telephone: 914.684.5800
www.brunschwig.com

Carlton V
D & D Building
979 Third Avenue, 15th Floor
New York, NY 10022
Telephone: 212.355.4525

Christopher Norman Inc.
41 West 25th Street, 10th Floor
New York, NY 10010
Telephone: 212.647.0303
www.christophernorman.com

Clarence House
211 East 58th Street
New York, NY 10022
Telephone: 212.752.2890
www.clarencehouse.com

Coraggio Textiles
1750 132nd Avenue NE
Bellevue, WA 98005
Telephone: 425.462.0035
www.coraggio.com

Cowtan & Tout
111 Eighth Avenue, Suite 930
New York, NY 10011
Telephone: 212.647.6900

Elizabeth Dow, Ltd.
155 Sixth Avenue, 4th Floor
New York, NY 10013
Telephone: 212.219.8822
www.edowltd.aol.com

Fortuny, Inc.
D & D Building
979 Third Avenue, 16th Floor
New York, NY 10022
Telephone: 212.753.7153
www.fortunyonline.com

Haas
50 Dey Street, Building One
Jersey City, NJ 07306
Telephone: 201.792.5959

Hinson & Company
2735 Jackson Avenue
Long Island City, NY 11101
Telephone: 718.482.1100

J. Robert Scott
500 North Oak Street
Inglewood, CA 90302
Telephone: 310.680.4300
www.jrobertscott.com

Jane Shelton
205 Catchings Avenue
Indianola, MS 38751
Telephone: 1.800.530.7259
www.janeshelton.com

Jim Thompson
1694 Chantilly Drive
Atlanta, GA 30324
Telephone: 1.800.262.0336
www.jimthompson.com/branch.html

Lee Jofa
225 Central Avenue South
Bethpage, NY 11714
Telephone: 1.888.LeeJofa
www.leejofa.com

Manuel Canovas
111 Eighth Avenue, Suite 930
New York, NY 10011
Telephone: 212.647.6900

Marvic Textiles
30–10 41st Avenue, 2nd Floor
Long Island City, NY 11101
Telephone: 718.472.9715

Nancy Corzine
256 West Ivy Avenue
Inglewood, CA 90302
Telephone: 310.672.6775

Nobilis
57-A Industrial Road
Berkeley Heights, NJ 07922
Telephone: 1.800.464.6670
www.nobilis.fr

Old World Weavers
D & D Buildings
979 Third Avenue
New York, NY 10022
Telephone: 212.355.7186

Osborne & Little
90 Commerce Road
Stamford, CT 06902
Telephone: 203.359.1500
www.osborneandlittle.com

Payne Fabrics
1000 Fountain Parkway
Grand Prairie, TX 75050
Telephone: 1.800.527.2517
www.westgatefabrics.com

Percheron
G6 Chelsea Harbour Design
Centre
London SW 10 OXE
ENGLAND
Telephone: 011.44.20 7349 1590

Peter Fasano, Ltd.
964 South Main Street
Great Barrington, MA 01230
Telephone: 413.528.6872

Pierre Frey, Inc.
12 East 33rd Street
New York, NY 10016
Telephone: 212.213.3099

Pollack & Associates
150 Varick Street
New York, NY 10013
Telephone: 212.627.7766

Prima Seta Silks/Jagtar & Co.
3073 North California Street
Burbank, CA 91505
Telephone: 818.729.9333

Quadrille
50 Dey Street, Building One
Jersey City, NJ 07306
Telephone: 201.792.5959

Robert Allen
55 Cabot Boulevard
Mansfield, MA 02048
Telephone: 1.800.240.8189

Rogers & Goffigon
41 Chestnut Street
Greenwich, CT 06830
Telephone: 203.532.8068

Rose Cumming
Fine Arts Building
232 East 59th Street, 5th Floor
New York, NY 10022
Telephone: 212.758.0844

Scalamandré
300 Trade Zone Drive
Ronkonkoma, NY 11779
Telephone: 631.467.8800
www.scalamandre.com

Schumacher Company
79 Madison Avenue, 14th Floor
New York, NY 10016
Telephone: 212.213.7900
www.fschumacher.com

Silk Trading Co.
360 South La Brea Avenue
Los Angeles, CA 90036
Telephone: 323.954.9280
www.silktrading.com

Travers
504 East 74th Street
New York, NY 10021
Telephone: 212.772.2778
www.traversinc.com

FURNITURE

Cameron Collection
150 Dallas Design Center
1025 North Stemmons Freeway
Dallas, TX 75207
Telephone: 214.744.1544

Charles P. Rogers
55 West 17th Street
New York, NY 10011
Telephone: 212.675.4400
www.charlesprogers.com

Dennis & Leen
8734 Melrose Avenue
Los Angeles, CA 90069
Telephone: 310.652.0855

The Farmhouse Collection, Inc.
807 Russet Street
Twin Falls, ID 83301
Telephone: 208.736.8700

Gregorius/Pineo
653 North La Cienga Boulevard
Los Angeles, CA 90069
Telephone: 310.659.0588

Hamilton, Inc.
8417 Melrose Place
Los Angeles, CA 90069
Telephone: 323.655.9193

Jane Keltner
94 Cumberland Boulevard
Memphis, TN 38112
Telephone: 1.800.487.8033
www.janekeltner.com

Michael Taylor Designs
1500 Seventeenth Street
San Francisco, CA 94107
Telephone: 415.558.9940

Niermann Weeks
Fine Arts Building
232 East 59th Street, 1st Floor
New York, NY 10022
Telephone: 212.319.7979
www.niermannweeks.com

Old Timber Table Company
908 Dragon Street
Dallas, TX 75207
Telephone: 214.761.1882

Patina, Inc.
351 Peachtree Hills Avenue NE
Atlanta, GA 30304
Telephone: 1.800.635.4365
www.patinainc.com

Plenty's Horn
15 County Road 2210
Pittsburg, TX 75686
Telephone: 903.856.3609

Randolph & Hein, Inc.
2222 Palou Street
San Francisco, CA 94124
Telephone: 415.864.3371

Lavender fills Provence's spring air with its scent, so not surprisingly it is the fragrance of choice in French homes and is widely available throughout France.

155

Reynière Workshop
142 Oak Road
Monroe, NY 10950
Telephone: 845.774.1541

Rose Tarlow/Melrose House
8454 Melrose Place
Los Angeles, CA 90069
Telephone: 323.653.2122

Shannon & Jeal
722 Steiner Street
San Francisco, CA 94117
Telephone: 415.563.2727

Smith & Watson
200 Lexington Avenue, Suite 801
New York, NY 10016
Telephone: 212.686.6444

Summer Hill, Ltd
2682 Middlefield Road
Redwood City, CA 94063
Telephone: 650.363.2600
www.summerhill.com

GARDEN ORNAMENTS

Elizabeth Street Garden &
Gallery
1172 Second Avenue
New York, NY 10021
Telephone: 212.644.6969

Lexington Gardens
1011 Lexington Avenue
New York, NY 10021
Telephone: 212.861.4390

Proler Oeggerli
2611 Worthington Street
Dallas, TX 75204
Telephone: 214.871.2233

Treillage, Ltd.
418 East 75th Street
New York, NY 10021
Telephone: 212.535.2288

IRONWORK

Brun Metal Crafts, Inc.
2791 Industrial Lane
Bloomfield, CO 80020
Telephone: 303.466.2513

Ironies
2222 Fifth Street
Berkeley, CA 94710
Telephone: 510.644.2100

Murray's Iron Work
5915 Blackwelder Street
Culver City, CA 90232
Telephone: 866.649.4766

156

Potter Art
4500 North Central Expressway
Dallas, TX 75206
Telephone: 214.821.1419
www.potterartmetal.com

E. Braun & Co.
717 Madison Avenue
New York, NY 10021
Telephone: 212.838.0650

Frette
799 Madison Avenue
New York, NY 10021
Telephone: 212.988.5221

Léron Linens
750 Madison Avenue
New York, NY 10021
Telephone: 212.249.3188

Peacock Alley
1825 Market Center Boulevard,
Suite 440
Dallas, TX 75207
Telephone: 214.744.0399

D. Porthault, Inc.
18 East 69th Street
New York, NY 10021
Telephone: 212.688.1660

Pratesi
4344 Federal Drive, Suite 100
Greensboro, NC 27410
Telephone: 336.299.7377

Yves Delorme
1725 Broadway
Charlottesville, VA 22902
Telephone: 1.800.322.3911
www.yvesdelorme.com

LIGHTING, LAMP, AND
CUSTOM LAMPSHADES

Ann Morris Antiques
239 East 60th Street
New York, NY 10022
Telephone: 212.755.3308

Bella Shades/Bella Copia
255 Kansas Street
San Francisco, CA 94103
Telephone: 415.255.0452

Chameleon
231 Lafayette Street
New York, NY 10012
Telephone: 212.343.9197

Marvin Alexander, Inc.
315 East 62nd Street, 2nd Floor
New York, NY 10021
Telephone: 212.838.2320

Murray's Iron Work
5915 Blackwelder Street
Culver City, CA 90232
Telephone: 310.839.7737

Nesle
151 East 57th Street
New York, NY 10022
Telephone: 212.755.0515
www.dir-dd.com/nesle.html

Niermann Weeks
Fine Arts Building
232 East 59th Street, 1st Floor
New York, NY 10022
Telephone: 212.319.7979

Panache
719 North La Cienega Boulevard
Los Angeles, CA 90069
Telephone: 310.652.5050

Paul Ferrante, Inc.
8464 Melrose Place
Los Angeles, CA 90069
Telephone: 323.653.4142

STONE AND TILE

Ann Sacks Tile & Stone
8120 NE 33rd Drive
Portland, OR 97211
Telephone: 1.800.969.5217
www.annsacks.com

Country Floors
15 East 16th Street
New York, NY 10003
Telephone: 212.627.8300
www.countryfloors.com

Brightening a landing off the entrance hall is a burnished metal sconce from the early nineteenth century that is one of a pair.

Paris Ceramics
151 Greenwich Avenue
Greenwich, CT 06830
Telephone: 1.888.845.3487
www.parisceramics.com

Walker Zanger
8901 Bradley Avenue
Sun Valley, CA 91352
Telephone: 877.611.0199
www.walkerzanger.com

TRIMMINGS AND
PASSEMENTERIE

Ellen S. Holt, Inc.
1013 Slocum Street
Dallas, TX 75207
Telephone: 214.741.1804

Houlès USA Inc.
8584 Melrose Avenue
Los Angeles, CA 90069
Telephone: 310.652.6171
www.houles.com

Kenneth Meyer Company
1504 Bryant Street, 3rd Floor
San Francisco, CA 94103
Telephone: 415.861.0118

Le Potager
108 West Brookdale Place
Fullerton, CA 92832

Leslie Hannon Custom
Trimmings
4018 East 5th Street
Long Beach, CA 90814
Telephone: 562.433.0161

Renaissance Ribbons
P.O. Box 699
Oregon House, CA 95961
Telephone: 530.692.0842
www.renaissanceribbons.com

Tassels & Trims
232 East 59th Street
New York, NY 10022
Telephone: 212.754.6000

West Coast Trimming
7100 Wilson Avenue
Los Angeles, CA 90001
Telephone: 323.587.0701

DIRECTORY OF INTERIOR DESIGNERS AND FIRMS

Trip Ayers
J. B. Ayers Antiques & Interiors, Inc.
2915 Fairfax Road
Cleveland Heights, OH 44106
Telephone: 216.397.0706
Facsimile: 216.397.3364

Gerrie Bremermann
Bremermann Designs
3943 Magazine Street
New Orleans, LA 70115
Telephone: 504.891.7763
Facsimile: 504.891.7765

Dan Carithers
Dan Carithers Design Consultant
2300 Peachtree Road NW
Suite B 201
Atlanta, GA 30309
Telephone: 404.355.8661
Facsimile: 404.355.7480

Sherry Hayslip, ASID and IIDA
Hayslip Design Associates
2604 Fairmount Street
Dallas, TX 75201
Telephone: 214.871.9106
Facsimile: 214.880.9049

Muriel Hebert Interiors
117 Sheridan Avenue
Piedmont, CA 94110
Telephone: 510.547.1294
Facsimile: 510.655.1509

Beverly Heil, Allied Member
ASID
Bev Heil and Associates
2905 North Henderson Avenue
Dallas, TX 75206
Telephone: 214.220.2015
Facsimile: 214.220.0602

Suzanne Kasler, ASID and IIDA
Suzanne Kasler Interiors
2300 Peachtree Road NW
Suite C 203
Atlanta, GA 30309
Telephone: 404.355.1035
Facsimile: 404.355.1025

John Kidd, Allied Member ASID
John Kidd Associates
5120 Woodway Road
Suite 7003
Houston, TX 77056
Telephone: 713.961.1888
Facsimile: 713.961.1912

Bobbie Dawn Lander
Sarah Lander Hast
Lander Mercantile
3602 Belt Line Road
Sunnyvale, TX 75182
Telephone: 972.226.6683
Facsimile: 972.226.2701

Betty Lou Phillips, ASID
Interiors by BLP
4278 Bordeaux Avenue
Dallas, TX 75205
Telephone: 214.599.0191
Facsimile: 214.499.0192

Christina Phillips, ASID
CMP Designs
5001 River Bluff Drive
Fort Worth, TX 76132
Telephone: 817.292.3994
Facsimile: 817.292.3694

Marilyn Phillips
Loren Interiors
1125 Riverbend Road
Houston, TX 77063
Telephone: 713.973.2466
Facsimile: 713.973.8859

Judy Robins
Judy Robins Interiors, Inc.
2165 East Alameda Avenue
Denver, CO 80209
Telephone: 303.777.8485
Facsimile: 303.722.7879

No problem if youngsters take their own sweet time coming to the table. The ice cream sodas and sundaes by Judy Blackman Floral Design, Dallas, are made of cut flowers. Handpainted table linens are from Peggy Walz in Manhattan. Pottery is made in Italy for Pottery Barn.

Richard Trimble, ASID and
Warren Wyatt
Richard Trimble & Associates, Inc.
3617 Fairmount Street
Suite 121
Dallas, TX 75219
Telephone: 214.526.5200

Carole D. Weaks, Associate IIDA
C. Weaks Interiors, Inc.
3133 Maple Drive
Suite 150
Atlanta, GA 30305
Telephone: 404.233.6040
Facsimile: 404.233.6043

DIRECTORY OF ARCHITECTS AND FIRMS

Richard Drummond Davis,
Architect
4310 Westside Drive
Suite H
Dallas, TX 75209
Telephone: 214.521.8763
Facsimile: 214.422.7674

Jerry Johnson, Architect
Caperton Johnson, Inc.
14860 Montfort Road
Dallas, TX 75240
Telephone: 972.991.7082
Facsimile: 972.991.2578

Anthony Paskevich, Architect
Anthony Paskevich & Associates
1708 Euclid Avenue
Cleveland, OH 44115
Telephone: 216.696.0916
Facsimile: 216.696.0968

Kurt Segerberg, Architect
Don Schieferecke, Architect
Segerberg Mayhew Architects
1000 South Frontage Road West
Suite 300
Vail, CO 81657
Telephone: 970.476.4433
Facsimile: 970.476.4608

DESIGNER CREDITS

Trip Ayers: 8–9, 104, 105, 118–119, 159

Gerrie Bremermann: 20, 21, 82–83, 127, 140

Dan Carithers: 19, 85, 88, 89, 109, 115, 132

Sherry Hayslip, ASID and IIDA: 101, 131

Muriel Hebert: front cover, 71, 80, 81, 96–97, 112, 139, 160

Bev Heil, Allied Member ASID: 12–13, 66, 68, 90, 99, 100, 108, 114, 117, 125, 128, 129, 133, 136, 138 center

Suzanne Kasler, ASID and IIDA: 16–17, 50–51, 60

John Kidd, Allied Member ASID: title page, 6, 45, 67, 70, 78, 79, 87, 102, 103, 110, 120, 121, 156, back cover

Bobbie Dawn Lander and Sarah Hast Lander: 5, 15, 49, 54, 55, 65, 74, 75, 126, 130 above, 137, 148 top

Betty Lou Phillips, ASID: endsheets, 27 below, 28, 29, 34 above, 53, 64, 92, 106, 107, 116, 138 bottom, 150–151, 157

Christina Phillips, ASID: 46, 47, 63, 73, 134–135

Marilyn Phillips: 48, 69, 122, 123

Judy Robins: 30–31, 35, 36

Richard Trimble, ASID and Warren Wyatt: 10, 32, 33, 42, 58, 59, 94, 95, 113, 138 top, 142–143, 145, 149

Carole Weaks, Associate IIDA: 40, 41, 43, 44, 62, 91

ARCHITECTURAL CREDITS

Richard Drummond Davis, Architect: 101, 131

Jerry Johnson, Architect: 32, 33, 42, 58, 59, 118, 138 top, 142–143, 145, 149

Anthony Paskevich, Architect: 8–9, 104, 105, 118–119, 159

Kurt Segerberg, Architect and Don Schieferecke, Architect: 29, 53, 92, 150–151

An espalier of miniature oranges climbs the wall of a French home.

159

Chinese-export porcelain and oversized Pierre Deux planters paired with topiary ivies reveal the home-owner/designer's delight in symmetry. A Japanese painting hangs above a table in the style of Louis XV. Vintage or not, Americans seek finely crafted furniture.